आनो भद्राः क्रतवो यन्तु विश्वतः

Let noble thoughts come to us from every side
—Rigveda 1-89-i

BHAVAN'S BOOK UNIVERSITY

General Editor
S. RAMAKRISHNAN

BODHI
BEAUTIFUL

**How to be a
Hindu
in America
by
LAWRENCE BROWN**

BHAVAN'S BOOK UNIVERSITY

BODHI BEAUTIFUL

How to be a Hindu in America

LAWRENCE BROWN

1999

BHARATIYA VIDYA BHAVAN
Kulapati Munshi Marg
Mumbai - 400 007

First Edition : 1999

Price : Rs. 90.00
$ 6.00

PRINTED IN INDIA

By Atul Goradia at Siddhi Printers, 13/14, Bhabha Building, 13th Khetwadi Lane, Mumbai 400 004 and published by S. Ramakrishnan, Executive Secretary, Bharatiya Vidya Bhavan, Kulapati Munshi Marg, Mumbai 400 007.

BODHI
means
ENLIGHTENMENT.

Dedication:

This book is dedicated to my wife, who has been my intellectual companion for 17 years. Also, I'm grateful to all the people who talk to me about their faiths and, in the process, help me to clarify my own. It's almost impossible to have a spiritual life without conversational companions. When they love you too and wish you well... what more could anyone ask?

Finally, deep gratitude to Shri Chand Kapur and Lila and Roshni Oberoi without whose encouragement and assistance this book could not have been printed in India.

1999

Lawrence W. Brown
44 Sylvan Drive
Hyannis, MA. 02601 USA
508-771-5096

TABLE OF CONTENTS

To the Reader, introduction

Things to Think About:

TO THE READER...

I was raised a Christian but couldn't stay with it. I liked women too much to prefer a Father-God and worshipped Nature before anyone told me it was idolatry. I was frightened by Christianity's violent history and turned off by fundamentalists who can't wait for the Christ of *Revelations* to come back, taking names and kicking butt.

So I joined the New Age Movement, attracted by its gentleness, openness, and lack of coercion. Eventually, I got hungry again. The New Age Movement may be a process – even a historic one – but it is not a destination. (Its points of departure are clearer than its destinations.) It lacks coherence and communion, things I've been increasingly needing. More and more, my wife and I are meeting New Age fundamentalists who have all the snobbery and exclusive possession of Truth that we've seen in so many Christians. So if someone asks my religion, I haven't known what to say.

What I've begun to realize is that I'm pretty much a Hindu. Not saying so out loud has been a bit of cowardice on my part because Americans have so little respect for Hinduism. *Buddhism* has earned itself a respected niche, but Hinduism is considered too barbarous and superstitious.

So it's weird being a Hindu in America.   The British used to call us *Hindoos* and spell it like they spelled *Voodoo*.   It made us even more exotic – or alien. Fine. So I'm a Hindoo. I suspect a lot of people in the New Age Movement are closet Hindoos. Maybe you're one too.

Are *you* a Hindoo too?
Suppose you believe in reincarnation. Suppose you believe that God can show up in many forms, not just one, and that all the world's religions are chasing after the same elusive thing. Maybe you see the natural world as being soaked in divine presence – so that God is not only outside nature, creating it, but *present* in the world around us. Maybe you believe that your soul is a spark of the same divinity that makes up the whole universe. Add to these ideas the thought that all that happens to us might be part of a divine lesson plan – and that maybe what's most important is not whether we survive the events of our lives but whether we *learn* from them.   Do *you* believe this stuff too? Then maybe you're a Hindu. If you don't come from India, maybe that just can't be helped.

Doesn't culture matter?
Wait a minute! Hinduism is not only a set of beliefs; it's a *tradition.* All the world's great religions are traditions with prayers and art and music and customs. All of those are a part of religion too.   There are ways people get married, for example.   The bride walks around

her husband three times... the wine glass is shattered under the heel... rice is thrown... an ox is beheaded and there's a huge feast. (They do that *somewhere*, don't they?) Surely you don't become a Christian or Muslim or Hindu or Jew like you become a Republican, do you... just like that? Just because you like the program?

Sure, we do. This is America. That's exactly how we do a lot of things. Is that a good thing about us? Maybe not. But we're also inventive. We jury rig "traditions" on a per-need basis. So if we cannot be from a Brahmin family or from the old village, *and yet we've found ideas of value,* we'll have to struggle to animate a foreign world-view with rituals and metaphors that speak to us where we are. If we already think we're Hindus – and we're in America – what else can we do? What else can we do if we discover what seems to be a body of truth than to believe it and try to put it in practice?

We can get our act together. We can find each other and offer some sense of community, find collective ways to meet the needs of others, think, discuss, help each other grow spiritually. The diversity of Hinduism offers hope that we can find a core of common beliefs without resorting to force or snobbery. We can even have a sense of humor. Maybe we can make ourselves at home.

Why aren't you a Buddhist?
I think being a Buddhist is a great idea, and it's gaining adherents these days. The wonderful advantage of Buddhism is that it has a master teacher – the Buddha himself. Buddha concentrated his efforts on the issue of suffering and how to deliver humanity from it. In this effort, he deliberately led the attentions of his followers away from the worship of gods into a practice of compassion and self-abnegation. It has many virtues.

Hinduism is more God-centered. You can be something of an atheist and still practice Buddhism successfully. That's one of its strengths. People who've been badly hurt or put off by the Western faiths with their Father God can find safe housing in Buddhism.

Hinduism can't do that. It doesn't offer you the Father God of Western faith, but there *is* a god at the center of everything. In Buddhism, you can have divinity (godliness) without deity (god). In Hinduism, you have both. So go, seek! Attempt to turn yourself into an instrument of search, a radio telescope scanning the heavens for celestial frequencies. It's a good thing to try.

Think of *all* the gods as study aids, signposts that point to our destination. But they are not the destination itself. Out on the edge of things, *Brahman* dances the Universe into being. But we cannot enfold the Infinite in a mind no bigger than a lunch box. We can only worship it.

the key point:
In the end, we do not pick our religion like we
pick a suit of clothes. We may, at first, sift
through the merchandise and try ideas on, but
finally we have to give ourselves away. We find
a religion like finding the right set of glasses.
At last, the world comes clear and we gaze and
we gaze... and we fall in love with what we see.
Love forces us to submit. *Without submission,
there is no faith.*

Somewhere, there is a vision like a clear lens
that clarifies our place in the world. Once we
have found it, there is only the choice between
clarity and obscurity. And clarity makes
demands. Whether it's Hinduism or Islam or
Judaism or Buddhism or Christianity – or
something else – *we must belong to it* or
nothing has happened. On this, all religions
agree.

Bodhi means *enlightenment*. It's a goal for us
Hindus, meaning it's the reward we seek for the
things we do. It's been an open invitation for
the last four thousand years: to love, create, and
understand things spiritually. Please stay with
me long enough to look into this.

INTRODUCTION TO PART ONE
- THINGS WE THINK ABOUT -

I'm writing this book to offer my readers a possible destination for their spiritual search. If you're just curious, that's fine too, but I've had to explain Hinduism to myself in a way that does justice to its ancient precepts and yet speaks to me where I live - and I am Western, born and raised American. I'm trying to figure out how to be a Hindu in America.

In organizing this project, there were two natural points of focus: *BELIEF* - the way a faith sees things... and *PRACTICE* - the things we do that enable us to be what God (as we see it) wants. This book is organized accordingly, starting with the beliefs that seem fundamental for Hindus.

Here's what we'll ask about first:

HOW DID ALL THIS GET STARTED?   We'll seek the roots of Hinduism in the shamanistic world view of Hunter/Gatherers.

WHO IS GOD? What do Hindus believe is behind the scenery of the Universe and how does it work?

WHO ARE WE? What does it mean to be a human being, from a spiritual point of view?

WHAT DOES GOD WANT? What are we here for; what (from a spiritual point of view) is the object of life?

WHAT DO THE IDEAS OF REINCARNATION AND KARMA MEAN? These are very difficult subjects, but they are so basic to the faith, we have to try to understand them.

So that's where we'll start.

- CHAPTER ONE -
The roots of Hinduism
a little background:

Not only is Hinduism the world's oldest major faith, its roots sink down into pre-history. When the Agricultural Revolution hit the Middle East 5 to 6 thousand years ago, a human rhythm a million years old was shattered. Imagine all of human history compressed into a single hour. In the hour of humanity's life on earth, we lived as hunter/gatherers for 59 minutes and 48 seconds. We've been farming for only 12 seconds. That's not a long time.

Once there were thousands of small bands of nomadic peoples - including some groups who had begun to do a little farming, raise a little livestock, do a little hunting, and share the results communally. Slowly a huge idea formed in old Sumer: *If leadership could be more authoritarian and less democratic, people could be compelled to labor at ambitious irrigation projects that could yield big food surpluses. Food surpluses would encourage population explosions. A huge mega-clan could overwhelm neighboring smaller groups and force them into slavery. (freeing up more local men for combat) Even more food could be grown. Additional slaves could build elaborate defensive fortifications to discourage reprisals... and so on.* It was a magnificent and horrible vision.

The leadership could enjoy a kind of personal power never before experienced by human beings. Hanging onto this power and passing it on to one's children would become an obsession. Both faith and the whole decision-making process would be warped into this obsession. What we call CIVILIZATION had begun.

The results might not be happier for the average human being, but this new kind of living would have one huge advantage: *it was more competitive.* Other tribes and clans would be forced to either imitate civilization in some way and compete on its terms - or be overwhelmed and perish. Ways of life that had served for millennia vanished. Among these would be a way of being religious in the world. That was *Shamanism.*

the world of the Shaman:
All the hunting and gathering groups left on Earth - and all we've ever known about - have seen their spiritual reality something like this:

It's nice to be a human being, but we play by the same rules as everything else in the world. What's true for the rock and the tree and the buffalo is true about us. If we think, those things think too. If we have a soul, so do they. For everything we can see with our eyes, there is a shadow reality of spirit which is just as real - it's just harder to see.

But it *can* be seen if you know how to look and if you have the knack for it. In most communities, there is at least one person who has that knack. That person is the SHAMAN.

what shamans do:
The shaman is a chameleon. He or she has learned how to leave the visible body and walk the land of the spirits. The dead are not far away. They are, in fact, at our very elbow. They yearn to be remembered, talked to, consulted, honored. When none of those things happen any longer, when the dead are forgotten, they fade away and eventually die a second death which is forever.

Then too, the shaman has the sick who need treatment with all the herbs to be learned about and, in dire cases, there are spirits who must be consulted for aid and advice. *(For Hindus, the multiplicity of spirits experienced by shamans evolved into belief in a multiplicity of gods.)*

Through drumming, chanting, drugs and dance, the shaman risks oblivion to leave this world and then return – over and over through a lifetime of service. Globally and historically, Shamanism has taken many forms. Each village, each people have had their own distinctive brand. Shamanism has always been pluralistic, diverse. But almost always there has been this respect for the spiritual dignity of the whole environment which is seen as being soaked in soul.

The agricultural societies that took up *feudal farming* – in which ownership of the land and its resources passed from the people into the hands of a small elite – needed religions to sanctify totalitarian rule. The universe of the Hunting/gathering people was too democratic. Creator gods who ruled like kings were needed – gods who would hand earthly power over to human beings, and then bless the power and affluence of a ruling class. In Egypt and Mesapotamia, all these things came to pass.

a different path:
In India around 2,500 B.C., a high civilization grew up along the Indus River. It had the most populous cities in the ancient world with organized housing in grid-like patterns, even sewers. Grain was stored in enormous brick beehive vaults – on hilltops where everyone could see them. These people had writing, too. We just can't figure out how to read it. What we can infer is that here, the world view of Shamanism was not abandoned. Instead, it evolved into Hinduism.

So what?
What's important here is that Hinduism seems to have developed right out of the shamanistic beliefs of Hunting / Gathering humanity. In the Middle East, the religions with a single Father God would put the Creator *outside* the world. The Creator would fashion the world and then give it to man "to have dominion over." So though God's fingerprints might be all over the world, God is not *in* the world.

Not only would the monotheisms destroy Hunting / Gathering people wherever they found them, they would make heresies out of their beliefs and destroy anyone in their own communities who held them. In Judaism, Christianity and Islam, nature is *not* divine and it's idolatry to believe it is. If you want to find God, you have to leave the world to do it.

This is not so in Hinduism.

the Aryans invade:
Around 2,500 B.C. a light-skinned people from southern Russia began to push their way into the mediterranean world and into India. They were a warlike people, bringing chariots into battle for the first time, and also iron. They pushed into Atlantic Europe, into Italy and Greece; they became the Hittites in the Middle East, the Iranians (Aryan-ians) and, around 1,500 B.C., they reached India.

Indo-European:
How surprised European scholars would be when they first studied Sanscrit, the language of India's scriptures, and found it to be a member of their own family of languages - "Indo-European. *Deus* means "God" in Sanscrit. *Zeus* means the same thing in Greek. *Pitar* means "father" in Sanscrit; *Pater* means the same in Latin. So "Father God" would be *ZeusPitar* - or *Jupiter* in Rome. And the Christians, whose seat of power settled in Rome, would start their Trinity with "God the Father..."

Theology gets around too.

the original Indians:
A smaller, dark-skinned people had been living in India. We call them "Dravidians." The first civilization in India had been their work. We can't read their writing, but their places for ritual bathing and positions for meditation suggest Hinduism's roots go back this far. One of their deities survived into later Hinduism, an Earth-goddess, *Ma*. One wonders whether Egypt's *Maat*, the Goddess of order and stability has the same root. "Ma" still means Mother.

synthesis:
Into this culture crashed the Aryans, wave after wave of them, from 1,500 B.C. on for another thousand years. The Dravidian civilization died quickly and a new civilization blended elements of the two cultures. It would become the civilization of India.

The newcomers had a more masculine view of the cosmos than the locals. In Aryan civilizations, the top gods would be male. Everywhere they went, goddess faiths were replaced or the goddesses were given inferior jobs in their new religions. This would happen in India also. The Goddess *Aditi (Infinity)* would give birth to a son and then fade to reappear as his daughter. It's the first application of the concept of reincarnation to the gods themselves

- and it conveniently repositioned Aditi in the new sexual order of Aryan India.

Religions, as expressions of human understanding and custom, evolve. Hinduism did not appear like Aphrodite from the sea foam - full-grown and complete. It evolved, as living things do. *All* religions evolve this way.

the caste system:
The Aryans considered themselves superior to the darker-skinned Dravidians. They set up what may be history's first system of aparthied. New laws forbade mixing of races and locked the Dravidians by job and by color into the social cellar. The concept of reincarnation would be drafted into social service to support aparthied: being born white and rich would be a reward for a virtuous prior life - and being born Dravidian was just desserts for past iniquity. Class and Karma were tangled so completely that India is only now beginning to extricate itself from caste. The swastika, an ancient Aryan symbol, would be dusted off by the Nazis as a symbol of racial supremacy - of a race of white conquerers. Some karma.

the evolution of the gods:
The oldest concept of divinity, beyond a belief in *divas* (nature spirits) and the souls of the departed, is that of the Goddess. It seems as old as homo sapiens, and goddess figurines date back at least 35 thousand years. The goddess is sometimes depicted on an elaborate birthing

chair - which, ironically, may have become the seat of masculine rule - the *throne*.

the first trinity:

The goddess concept gradually expanded to include Her in three persons: the *Maiden*, promising pleasure and potential... the *Mother*, fruitful and nurturing... and the *Crone*, signifying both wisdom and death - nature reclaiming its own. Much later, Christianity would seek to exterminate goddess faith. The Maiden, freely sexual, became the harlot. The Crone became the witch and was consigned to the fire. The Mother they could use. Hinduism would use all three.

Iditi we've already mentioned, also *Ma*. The Crone appears in several guises. *Kali* is best known in the West. She's death but more accurately, the *recycler*, pictured with a string of skulls around her waist.

Gods and goddesses would stream into Hinduism from every quarter. What Westerners will often miss with ancient religions is that the fantastical representations of many ancient divinities could be taken literally by the unsophisticated and be understood as metaphors by an inner circle. A god with many arms suggests power. Many faces suggests vigilance - or a more complex idea still: that the many faces we see are, in reality, the same god.

the second trinity:
Eventually a creator god became the centerpiece of Hindu faith. This was *Brahma*. Then another idea rose up beneath this one: that the underlying reality behind the universe was incomprehensible. Even the gods themselves would be the creation of *BRAHMAN* with an N. We'd have reality in escalating layers of enormous majesty ascending beyond human imagination. The gods beneath *BRAHMAN* would have their stories but would also represent some abstract quality of the Divine. The uppermost tiers of Hindu divinity would look like this:

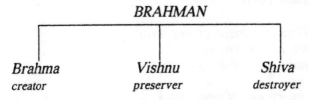

BRAHMAN

Brahma
creator

Vishnu
preserver

Shiva
destroyer

Here's the concept of reincarnation in celestial form - and it's all divine. God the creator *(Brahma)* sends the material universe spinning and then goes to sleep. God the preserver *(Vishnu)* maintains the creation in balance and then, when its time for the closing of the age, God the destroyer *(Shiva)* inhales reality back into himself, wakes up Brahma, and the whole cycle begins again. We live in a reincarnated universe. Of all the ancient faiths, only Hinduism sees the universe in galactic terms - a plurality of worlds.

Where do these gods come from? Some, like Shiva, seem to come from the original Dravidian culture. Others, like Brahma, seem to have come in with the Aryans. *BRAHMAN*, the God of gods, seems to be a collective insight. Others, like the popular elephant-headed god *of* wisdom *Ganesa*, is really old - maybe 4,500 years old - pre-Aryan.

God incarnate:
Then there is Krishna. Krishna is a god with lots of stories. He's a prodigious lover, irresistible to maidens (milkmaids) when he plays his flute. But he's more. Krishna represents the gods' mercy on Earth. He's a god incarnate - made flesh.

"When goodness grows weak,
when evil increases,
I make myself a body.

In every age, I come back
to deliver the holy
to destroy the sin of the sinner,
to establish righteousness." says Krishna
in the BHAGAVAD-GITA. This is why Hindus can accept the divinity of Jesus. (The word *Christ*, Greek for "savior", could be a linguistic cousin to *Krishna*.) Hinduism *expects* gods to take human form.

It's this very plasticity of the Divine that's so off-putting to Westerners. There's even a pyramid in India swarming with sculpted statues of divinities – *hundreds* of them! If all of them are, in some way, representations of the God of gods, how can we ever get to the bottom of it all?

A child in ancient times asked his father what the world rested on. "It's on the back of a giant tortoise," his father said.
"And on what is the tortoise standing?" he asked.
"On the back of another tortoise."
"And on what is *that* standing?"
His father anticipated the line of questioning. "Look," he said, "it's tortoises all the way down.

Is that how it is, or is God at the bottom of it all? And if God is at the bottom of it all, exactly who or what is that?

- CHAPTER TWO -
WHO IS GOD?

> The next thing we have to do
> is ask is, "WHO IS GOD?"
> Where does the Hindu answer
> come from and what is it?
> What does the idea of many gods
> mean, and are the Hindu deities
> necessary to Hinduism?
>
> The answers are fundamentally
> different than what most of us
> have grown up with in the West,
> but you might find them attractive.

In Hinduism, everything in the world is a manifestation of God. (Brahman) The world is *made* of God.

In Hinduism, there are several very specific names for God as the ground of all being, as the object of worship, and as the divine element present in all things. Whenever I use the term God in talking to you, I will be referring to the concepts of Hinduism, not the Father God of the West.

a way to see things:
Imagine an enormous galaxy far off in space.

Seen from a distance, it is a spinning pinwheel of radiance. The light is most brilliant at its center, where it seems fused into one immense ball. Is it a ball or the collected illuminations of a billion suns? From where we are, we cannot tell.

Spinning away from it is a continual blur of stars. In one sense, each star is a thing unto itself; but we can also see that each star has spun from the whole and is made of what the whole is made from.

When some of these stars mature, they will become solar systems, with planets and possibly unique life-forms. When that happens, we may forget where they came from and what they're really made of.

So it is with God. Everything, whatever its form, is made of God. God is not contained in *any* single piece of reality, but in *every* thing we see, we see the face of God.

So should we worship everything we see? Should we worship a leaf? If you're a Hindu, why not? You can start anywhere. Just try to remember that the destination is always Brahman whirling beyond our sight, incomprehensibly spinning stars into the night. That is God.

the edge of the envelope:
Of course, if that is what God is, our imaginations are going to fail us - and language is too. Part of being a Hindu is being suspicious of language. It's a kind of modesty lacking in the practitioners of many religions. Hindus cheerfully admit right off that any description or explanation one could come up with is inadequate. The galactic picture I just offered you is only useful if it points you in the right direction.

The more sure a religion is that it's got the Divine contained in the volumes of its scripture, the more apt it is to be brutal and repressive. We Hindus don't want to be brutal and repressive, so we remind ourselves and our listeners that *language can only be helpful, never definitive*. For us, with minds no bigger than a lunchbox, the Ultimate is unknowable.

For help, we get the little gods.
Because Hinduism has its roots in Shamanism, it never lost the local colors that each community used to paint its pictures of the Divine. It simultaneously blesses each faith and demotes them to a set of sign-posts pointing to a God beyond anyone's comprehension. In addition, Hinduism itself has room for all sorts of understandings. There are no Hindu heresies.

Here's the problem: If we imagine a god with a comprehensible face, logic tells us it can't be what God's really like. If we can only have God at the edges of the Universe, where is the love and redemption we need? Who is there to see us and care about us? A distant and disinterested god is like having no god at all.

the root of polytheism:
Brahman may touch our minds, but not fill our hearts. So just as Brahman creates worlds, so Brahman creates gods. We need them. Think of all the different cultures. Think of all the different kinds of people there are... all the different capacities for thinking in abstractions. How could one god make sense and speak to them all? Other faiths may dream of that blessed day when all humanity fits into a single spiritual mold, thinks the same thoughts. Hinduism doesn't hold its breath.

The supernatural experiences of every culture suggest spiritual presences are always close to us. These are not the God of gods; they feel local and personal. Hindus began thinking of them as gods with a small *G*.

If we feel the presence of somone who has previously died... if we stand at the foot of a mountain as the sun sets behind it or feel the presence of Divinity in a shaft of sunlight, does it have to be the Lord of the Universe every time? Often, it doesn't feel like it, but we know we felt *something* divine.

Does God have a gender?
If you think about it, it's a silly question. Does

God have balls or walk around the vacuum of space on two feet? The world's monotheisms have insisted on God the Father for reasons far more social than theological. Surely there is equal divinity in the feminine as in the masculine, but the God of Gods has either all genders or none. What do you wish to see?

Now wait a minute! Is the God of gods making up the company of Heaven - or are *we* doing it? To which the Hindu replies, "What difference does it make?" The point of all religions is to make spiritual progress. Does the worship of Christ or Allah, or following the Commandments assist us in making progress? It certainly offers us the chance. So it's fine. Though the propositions of faiths often differ, in another sense, they're all true. The gods of our imagining carry us all to the feet of the God of Gods. God is everywhere, so the search can start anywhere you are.

This open-mindness enfuriates fundamentalists who insist that their scripture and their scripture alone is the true revelation from the one true God. The friendly Hindu equality relegates them all to the same plane.

If you want to be a Hindu in America, be prepared to irritate all fundamentalists without ever pleasing any of them. You won't be able to help it. Hinduism is the opposite of fundamentalism. That's one of my favorite reasons for liking it.

Is spiritual pluralism an absurdity?
If different religions make wildly contradictory
claims, how can Hindus say with Gandhi that "all
religions are true"? We do it by remembering
what religions are for. They exist to promote
the spiritual progress of their members. In the
absence of an impartial authority to rule on faith
disagreements, we simply applaud the spiritual
accomplishments of people of every faith and
pray that violence doesn't intrude. With this
approach, it is maybe easier for Hindus and
Buddhists to be tolerant than for those of any
other faith.

Are the Hindu gods necessary to Hinduism?
This is an important question. The Hari Krishna
movement has for years attempted to interest
Americans in Hinduism by offering the full
pantheon of traditional gods represented in
traditional Indian art. This has been too difficult
for most Americans to accept, but I have come
to believe that though the expressions of God
are cultural, the *presence* of God is not. Those
of us born outside the mother culture of India
must, with care and gratitude, try to lift the
universal insights of Hinduism from their
cultural setting.

This is not to say the Hindu gods are
meaningless here. To the contrary; if you've
been reading this and finding the ideas congenial
to your understanding, a little research into the
central deities of Hinduism is a logical growth
step. But if we understand the gods to be

among the countless faces of the same central God of gods, then we are free to look into the faces that are most meaningful to us. If Christ touches you more readily than Krishna, that has to be all right. If Christians can't return the largess, that's *their* problem, not yours.

Hinduism shares with Shamanism experiences of the Supernatural that are local and personal. What the West has called angels, ghosts and devils, Hindus have called gods. The difference between all these is more semantic than actual and religions in the West and East know better than to confuse angels, spirits, and ghosts with the God of gods. Still, Hinduism insists that whenever you've experienced the Supernatural, you've touched the face of God – even if you couldn't see it.

So what have we said here?
1) We've said that *Hinduism seems to be a sophistication of Shamanism.* If you've been interested in Native American or African beliefs, there is much here that deepens or compliments these traditions.

2) In Western monotheisms, God isn't *in* the world. In Hinduism, as in most Shamanism, *the Universe is divine. God is IN it as well as outside it. If it's real, it's God.*

3) Finally, *since the God of gods is beyond our understanding, we use the gods of our imagination to make spiritual progress, as objects of reverence and points of focus.* That's the best we can do, so it has to be all right.   This understanding dignifies all faiths, even when they differ.

If all this sounds reasonable - especially if it sounds more reasonable than anything *else* you've heard, maybe you're a Hindu.

WHO GOD IS, *from the SVETASVATARA UPANISHAD*

> God is, in truth, the whole Universe. Without hands, he holds all things; without feet, he runs everywhere. Without eyes he sees all things, without ears, all things he hears.
>
> It is not speech we should want to know; we should want to know the speaker.
> It is not mind we should want to know,
> WE SHOULD WANT TO KNOW THE THINKER.

- CHAPTER THREE -
WHO ARE WE?

> *"What is man, oh Lord,"* the psalmist wrote,
> *"that Thou should be mindful of him?"* That
> is our next logical question. What does it mean
> to be a human being?

We are embodied souls.
That is the fundamental truth about us. If it's
hard to really pin down what the God of gods
is... not really this, not really that, not really
anything we can comprehend... then the same
must be said for ourselves. We are not of this
world, yet we are in the world. Here we go
again: *language is not going to be up to really
explaining this to us.* So we'll have to be careful
and patient with the attempts of people who try to
teach us about our spiritual selves. We'll have to
remember also to stay humble. Excessive
certainty is the enemy of spiritual growth. Pride
kicks in too easily for our own good.

your deepest self
Your deepest self is the one that lasts. If, as
Hindus believe, the soul has its cycles, just as
nature has, then your soul and your ego cannot
be the same thing. Consider: out of the ocean of
soul that is the source of everything, a droplet of
spirit enters the world. It cycles through
existance and, at the moment, it's you. When

you die, it will shed your body like a suit of clothes and become someone else. In other words, the soul sheds egos and puts on new ones — so, though it's natural to become attached to our ego, that attachment distracts us from remembering what we really are.

What's the point?
Why do Hindus think it happens this way? By observing nature, I think. If I'm right, Hinduism evolved out of Shamanistic traditions that were close to nature. The cyclical view of things just made sense — that if nature worked in cycles, then soul did also.

Is it the only sense we could make? Of course not. Judaism saw time as linear, historical: history has a beginning and an end. Meanwhile, we are headed somewhere. This view of how time (and history) works laid the foundation for Christianity and Islam — and became the world-view of the West. The idea of *progress* is Western — and originally Jewish. That view of the world makes just as much sense as the cyclical one does. Ask a Jew why the universe works the way it does and you'll hear that *it's just how it is* — that God made it that way... which is also the Hindu's answer. In the end, you'll be drawn to the world view that speaks to you most deeply. That's how it works for everybody.

But who's got the right answer?
God knows. Literally. A little humility would go a long way here, starting with me. I can't tell

you because I don't know. As things have made a certain sense for me, I am sharing that sense with you and claiming nothing more. I hope that's O.K.

> The answer to our very deepest questions is always that *it's just how it is*. God cannot download cosmic truth into minds the size of a lunchbox. For this very reason, no one has the right to impose his understanding on the rest of us saying, "That's just how it is." Only God gets to say that. Where can you hear the voice of God? Inside yourself. Hindus believe there's a piece of God in there. Listen to that.

Unifying East and West:
There's a way to visualize how the linear and cyclical understandings of time could be combined – and it uses a symbol basic to Hindu thinking: the wheel. The wheel doesn't only revolve. When it touches the ground, *it moves!* There can be forward progress to a cyclical motion. The soul *is*, in fact, headed somewhere. It's headed towards *enlightenment*. What is enlightenment? It's knowing and living in the knowledge that you're really a soul.

being a soul in the world:
Meanwhile, we have a problem. If the world is made of God, and the soul *is* of God, then aren't souls and the world made of one and the same thing. And if they are, what's this Hindu talk

about Maya, illusion, Samsara?   What's the problem?

the solid soul:
Hinduism and Buddhism have traditionally viewed the world as *Samsara* – as a place of transitions, of appearences or illusions. The soul is not some ephemeral kind of ghost inhabiting the world of solid objects – quite the reverse! It is *soul* that's real and the world that's ephemeral. It's the soul that survives, after all, while everything that appears to be solid passes away.

So the Hindu might offer you this example: *A person falls asleep and dreams of a sinking ship full of passengers screaming for help.   Waking from sleep, the dreamer is full of anxiety for the fate of these unfortunate people until the sunlight and singing birds announce that in reality there is no ship and no passengers... just a dream, an illusion.   IRONICALLY, THIS PERSON, NO LONGER ASLEEP, IS UNAWARE THAT THE WORLD IS SIMPLY A MORE COMPLEX DREAM WHICH THE UNAWAKENED <u>SOUL</u> IS HAVING.* We call this dreamworld in which our unawakened souls are all enmeshed: SAMSARA.

I confess to having a real problem with this understanding. Maybe it's a cultural thing, but if I'm going to be a Hindu in America, I may need to develop an understanding that speaks to me where I am.

reconciling soul and substance:
If the soul is God and the world is really made of
God too, then I should love the god in all things.
If the soul and the world are both made of God,
then the Divine should not distrust itself. *We
don't need to awaken from dreaming that the
world is real; we need to awaken from the illusion
that our egos are real, that we are separated from
the world and separated from God.* We wake up
spiritually in the act of loving.

what our egos are for:
In loving, we can't escape the impression that it
is *we* - our egos - that are doing the loving.
Who is doing the loving, after all, if not our
selves?

> It is our souls that are straining to love the
> world. Our souls love the world *through
> our egos* because, while we are here in the
> world of Samsara, there is no other way for
> them to do it. *The world suffers in Samsara
> because most egos do <u>not</u> love the world
> but seek only themselves.*

Imagine lovers in overcoats holding each other
close. They yearn to feel their flesh pressed
against each other, but there is all this fabric in
the way. So it is for loving souls with layers of
ego in their way.

What Samsara is:
Samsara is the experience of being an enduring soul in a world that is continually coming into being and passing away. Our souls are not separated from the world because they are superior somehow. (We can avoid the spiritual snobbery here. We're all made of God.) *Our souls feel estranged from the world because they experience time differently, because they endure while the objects of their love perish.* That is why there is sadness in Samsara.

So what are we doing here?
We are here to learn how to unify soul and substance. We can only accomplish this by loving what is in the world. Knowing that our souls can take nothing with them, we need to love without selfishness. This is hard for us and may take lifetimes of practice.

1) First, we need to simply accept that selfless loving is what we are here to learn. *We love things which, because we are soul, we cannot possess.* We learn to do this joyfully.

2) We need discipline and concentration to stay with this effort and check ourselves all the time so that the allure of power and greed don't deflect us from our task.

3) We need to remember all the time that we are souls.

4) We need to remember God and seek God in all things.

So *what are we?* We are what attempts all this.

ON THE SOUL, from the *BHAGAVAD - GITA...*

*Worn out garments are shed by the body;
worn out bodies are shed by the dweller
within the body.*

*Knowing it birthless...
knowing it deathless...
knowing it endless...
dream not the power is yours
to command it.*

*Not wounded by weapons, not burned by fire,
not dried by the wind, not wetted by water,
such is the Atman. (God within you)
Not dried nor wetted,
not burned nor wounded,
innermost element everywhere, always,
Being of beings, changeless, eternal,
for ever and ever.*

- CHAPTER FOUR -
What Does God Want?

> This is another way of asking what we are
> supposed to be doing – and thinking about. By
> "God" I don't necessarily mean the Father God
> of the Western faiths, but if Jews, Christians,
> or Muslims care to listen in, I don't think our
> answers will be that different.

What are we supposed to be thinking about?
First of all, I think we're supposed to be
remembering that we're souls in body suits. We
see the world differently when we look at reality
through a spiritual lens. It's easy to be distracted
by ego, by both pains and pleasures... so we have
to accept a mental discipline of constantly
remembering what we are and checking up on our
rememberance all the time. This is important.

How do we do this?
Ritual, prayer, and meditation are the best ways
to do it. Hinduism has rich traditions in all three.
The *Upanishads* is an ancient collection of Hindu
prayers availible in bookstores and you can find
more in the religion section of any large
bookstore. You can adapt prayers from other
traditions and make up your own, too. What is
key is that *when routine space is made for
spiritual practice, it helps us remember that we
are souls.* Mohammed knew what he was doing
when he set aside 5 intervals for prayer every day

for everybody. We need spiritual routines.

We need to remember God.
The Muslims refer often to *the constant rememberance of God*. If we are souls in bodysuits, we need to remember where we came from. We need a practice that has some chance of competing against the hurricane of sound and stimulation coming in from Samsara, from the world of the senses. *"Be still,"* says the psalmist, *"and know that I am God."*

The traditional Hindu form of stillness is meditation.
If prayer is speaking, meditation is listening. Our minds are chaotic, noisy places. It's amazingly difficult to get our brains to shut up. Usually, we need a point of focus. For thousands of years, Hindus have used *breath* to do this. Just focus on your own breathing, being attentive to the breath coming in and out. When thoughts zoom through, smile at them inwardly, then kindly show them the door. Inhale... exhale. Let the distractions go. They'll keep zooming in, of course - like comets. Practice holding the door for them so they can soar right on through.

Maybe you can think of your mind as a cavernous room, a planetarium speckled with stars - or the emptiness of space. Look around in there but keep it quiet, with the distant sighing of your breath in and out like surf on a distant beach.

What if nothing happens?
That's OK. So you had a few minutes to stretch your bones on the cosmic beach. Maybe after a while, when you inspect the place inside your head, you'll notice a package lying around. Funny, it wasn't there last time you looked. It seems to be for you. Maybe it's from God.

looking for God:
You're not stuck inside your head, you know. You can leave. Maybe you can go looking for God. You begin the same way... quiet mind, open space expanding. Let it get dark in there with just the distant surf of breathing, slow and rhythmic.

Now the vault of your skull opens like huge doors and beyond the doors, it is night; it is space. Out you drift, out the doors. There's no sound but your distant breathing. You look around. It's neat out here. Remember in chapter one the image of Brahman as the whirling fountain of light, spinning out galaxies and worlds? Imagine it from a distance as just a speck of light. Let yourself sail off in search of that light. Slowly, as you approach, you begin to appreciate its immensity. This light is God. What does the face of God look like? Go find out.

A skeptic will argue that, of course, you're not leaving your mind at all, that you're just *thinking* all this - as I am writing it. Fine. Nothing any religion has to say will ever dislodge the skeptic from his skepticism. It is the skeptic's faith that there's nothing there. Don't worry about it. Go seek. Learn what you learn; know what you know. Leave the business of conversion to others. What you are, you are. If people have a soul and don't know it, it will be their *souls*, not you, who will eventually convince them differently.

There's no such thing as *saving* someone by changing his theology.

In general, while Hindus know how lost and confused we can be, they also know that we're souls in body suits, that we are manifestations of God. Consequently, Hindus believe we can accomplish great things when we set our minds to it. In this respect, Hinduism can be amazingly optimistic about our spiritual growth.

prayer:
If meditation is listening, prayer is speaking. We, in the West, do a lot more speaking than listening. A lot of prayer in all traditions treats God like some sort of king who appreciates fawning and flattery. So most hymns are loaded with praise, sprinkled with occasional gratitude, and burdened with requests. Speaking just personally here, I've liked some of the music and been embarrassed by most of the lyrics.

What is prayer and ritual for?
If the object of any religion is the spiritual growth of its members, then the object isn't to flatter God but increase our godliness, to heal and

comfort others, and gain in understanding... or to *remind* ourselves that these things need doing. We ask for insight or the strength to do right. We ask for the health and peace of others or for their spiritual growth.

Prayer is spoken compassion. We can look at our prayers, the ones we borrow and the ones we make up, in this light.

OM:
The OM chant is a kind of spiritual dial-tone that holds our lines open for a higher frequency. It's a way of jamming the lower frequencies to keep out distractions. In meditation, it transforms our breath from the surf on a distant beach to an internal hum of Heaven. You'll feel silly at first, but try closing your eyes and toning a deep OM during each slow exhalation. Hold the note and let it fill your skull and resonate in your sinuses. Try it for 5 minutes, doing nothing else. See what you think. If something good seems to be happening, even if you're not sure what it is, make it a routine. I've done it in the shower to start my day.

Hindus have been experimenting with stuff like this for thousands of years and settled on OM as the ideal mantra. Trust that they're on to something.

pathways to God:
Hindus have a nice understanding approach to
human beings. They avoid the one-size-fits-all
approach so popular with fundamentalists and
instead recognize that there are different kinds of
people. Different people need different
approaches – and Hinduism offers them different
paths.

> *Fundamentalists tend to believe that Heaven has*
> *but one door; Hindus believe there are many.*
> *One destination; many paths; many doors.*
> *"Whatever road men may take," says Krishna in*
> *the Bhagavad Gita, "all roads lead to Me." This*
> *understanding is the basis of religious tolerance.*

In the end, the goal of Hinduism is *enlightenment,*
which is complete understanding of our spiritual
identity and living accordingly. There are several
ways to get there.

the path of meditation:
This is ideal for contemplative souls, introverts
who already turn inward almost instinctively. In
other words, your mind can be a path to God.
People taking this approach need to make a real
routine out of meditation, a serious commitment.

the path of devotion (prayer and ritual):
Traditional Hinduism has long honored this path.
The Buddha worried that it could become empty
pageantry without increasing goodness or
insight. For an American, not born to the

Hindu prayers and rituals, this would be a hard path to follow. One might *feel* very Hindu and exotic, but not get far... I worry about that.

the path of renunciation:
Remember, in traditional Hinduism, the object is to reach enlightenment and escape Samsara, the cycle of rebirth. Perhaps the world will not let go of you until you let go of it. Imagine you're on a train. It travels a huge loop, returning after many years to the same station – its only stop. If you want to get off the train, you must be ready, because it stops for only a minute. So if you really want to get off, you can get off.

But if you've just met someone attractive; if you're in the middle of a card game or an argument or an interesting discussion and you want to see how things turn out... or you're eating or maybe asleep... or you're trying to get off with all your baggage and you can't move it through the train fast enough... the train will stop for its minute, one or two people will get off, and you're off for another cycle. The path of renunciation requires that you've absolutely had enough of the train and you want off more than you want on.

It is traditionally thought that elderly people are ideally suited for the path of renunciation. Been there; done that; ready to get off for good. In any case, the path of renunciation cannot be the path of the materialist or the sensation seeker – which means a lot of Americans would find this a difficult path.

the path of compassion:
We said earlier that maybe it's not the world but the *ego* that is in our way. So maybe you can beat the ego into shape by going on a starvation diet – or maybe you can accomplish the same thing by trying to feed the world.

The path of compassion requires us to see how everyone is struggling in Samsara. We're all souls that give themselves to temporal things that perish. We're all confused by desire and loss. So our heart goes out to everyone and everything in the world of Samsara. And when we do this, where is the ego?

This is not a ritual thing particularly. There are few bells and whistles, no special clothes to wear, no bumper stickers. Just openness... empathy... cheerfulness...kindness...service. How to begin? Just try to warm and illuminate the room you're in. Practice kindness all the time, each chance you get until you become a human lighthouse, an incandescent bulb. When we live this way instinctively, automatically, God teaches us everything we need to know.

Bodhi means enlightenment. A *Bodhisattva* (bo-dee-*sat*-vah) is someone who has attained enlightenment and is therefore released from Samsara – but cannot bear to leave others behind.

Hindus believe humanity is not left to struggle in Samsara alone. We have the sense of spiritual presences that feel personal... here to help us. There are individuals who are spiritually advanced. There are giants of ,the intellect, paragons of prayer and holiness, and the bodhisattvas who are in the world to love the world. To achieve spiritual growth, we need to really want to. We need spiritual ambitions. We need role models who point to spiritual destinations. When we embark on our journey consciously and with determination... and when we learn how to be souls in the world, we gain enlightenment. That is what God wants.

So what do we understand here?

1) *We are souls in body suits.*

2) *We need ritual, prayer, and meditation to help us remember who we are.*

3) *There are spiritual paths suited to our temperments and intellects. These are: meditation, devotion, renunciation, and compassion. Heaven has many doors with many ascending pathways to it.*

4) *Our special goal is enlightenment - knowing we are souls on Earth and acting accordingly every day.*

ON JOY, *taken from several UPANISHADS*

> *Brahman is joy: FROM JOY ALL BEINGS HAVE COME, BY JOY THEY LIVE AND UNTO JOY THEY ALL RETURN.*
>
> *Where there is joy, there is creation.*
> *Where there is no joy, there is no creation.*
> *Know the nature of joy.*

- CHAPTER FIVE -
KARMA AND THE WHEEL OF LIFE

Crucial to Hinduism and Buddhism – and to much New Age belief too – is the belief in reincarnation. This concept is basic to both faiths. With reincarnation comes the idea of KARMA. What is all this about – and what are the implications if we accept these ideas as true?

As you can see so far, we're still trying to make sense out of a tradition that has some real differences from the faiths most of us have grown up with. As in any religion, we have *ideas* and *practices* – what we believe and what we do. We're winding up the *ideas* phase with this discussion.

the wheel of life – *spiritual recycling:*
If nature works in cycles, Hindus believe the soul does too. From the great ocean of reality that is Brahman come droplets of soul that appear as living things in the physical world. As beings age and die, their spiritual essences persist to become new life. Through life after life, the soul grows towards self-awareness – also towards *universal* awareness.

the worm in the apple:

Notice here the seeds of a problem: *as the soul grows towards self-awareness, its ego grows more distinct.* It has an ever clearer and more detailed sense of itself as a separate being. And it grows towards *universal* awareness... towards the understanding of itself as a spiritual being – as a part of Brahman, a part of God and the whole creation. In other words, *as the soul evolves, it grows in its capacity to grasp both error and truth.* How will it know which way to go?

the cosmic practical joke:

Hindus believe that the soul in Samsara is both confused and surrounded by confusion concerning its true nature. Isn't that a dirty trick for Brahman to do? (Isn't original sin a dirty trick for Jehovah to do?) All religions have to - at some point - interpret the ridiculousness of human existence as some kind of cosmic challenge, as some kind of maze we have to find our way out of. Humanity put *itself* into a historical maze when we stopped living by the rhythms and the laws of nature. We have assumed that the perversity of human life is somehow the doing of the Gods and that it is our spiritual task to find our way out - to be *saved.*

Well. We may be in a maze of our own making... yet escaping from it may still be a spiritual project. The maze seems so impenetrable, it seems that God made it for us, but we might well be wrong about that. When we were creatures of nature, we mustn't have been any more confused about how to live than a buffalo or an owl. Now we are apart from nature – and *now* we are confused. Whose fault is that?

Karma:
In any case, Hindus have a name for the maze; they call it *Samsara*. According to their general intuition, it's no accident that you and I find ourselves in Samsara. It's cause and effect. The system of cause and effect, working at the spiritual level, is called *Karma*. We can get into more detail, but *the essence of Karma is the conviction that the past is operative in the present.*

1) *While it has been the common belief in the West that we get one life on Earth and then spend eternity in Heaven or Hell, Hinduism (and Buddhism) believe that your soul returns to the flesh over and over in the cycle of rebirth. (reincarnation)*

2) *There is a system of cosmic cause and effect that determines the conditions of our lives on Earth. This is called Karma. We seem to have lessons to learn and keep returning until we have learned them.*

That, in very brief, is the outline of our work here. But rebirth (reincarnation) and Karma are complex ideas with lots of wrinkles in them. It's not just splitting hairs to go into these ideas more deeply. If the foundations of a faith don't make

sense - *don't help make the world make sense* -
we're wasting our time.

*When people try to believe something that doesn't
make sense, it takes a lot of energy. The more
irrational the belief, the more energy it takes to
believe it and the uglier and more coercive their
religion gets.*

When faith *illuminates* life, there is some
sweetness to it. A faith that makes sense and
seems to check out has a chance to grow without
violence. That's the kind of faith Hindus want.

So we're going to wrestle with these difficult ideas
for a while. Monks and priests in India and Tibet
spend *years* on these concepts, so we won't make
much of a dent from their point of view.

How do we know what happens when we die?
We don't.

**Then where do all the fancy theories come from -
and why believe them?**
We have an interesting body of lore from near-
death experiences suggesting experience continues
after the brain flatlines. If there are no brain-
waves, exactly what is it that's having experience?

We have to suppose that ancient peoples also had
near-death experiences, and told stories and
thought deeply about them. Drug and dance-
induced states can also take us out of our bodies.

Shamans have done this long before recorded history... and then there have been all manner of reported encounters with the souls of the dead. All these, taken together, must have formed the basis for humanity's conviction that the soul/mind persists after the death of the body. Occasional flash-back memories of past lives would suggest reincarnation.

This belief in some kind of life after death is at the core of almost all the world's great religions. *All additional details are the product of reflection and conjecture attaching themselves to that core belief.* What else could we do but reflect and conjecture about it? Different cultures would naturally have different starting and ending points.

What are the world's various beliefs on this?
NO AFTERLIFE. Judaism.
God is the soul for the Universe. We get *life*, god's unique gift, and instructions on how to be human beings. (the Law)

RESURRECTION: Christianity
Traditional belief is that the souls of the dead sleep until Christ's return when they will rise to face God's judgment and reward.

IMMORTALITY: Islam, some Christians, and many other ancient religions now defunct.
When the body dies, the soul is judged and spends eternity in a paradise or place of

punishment. Shamanism sees souls residing in a shadowland close to us but not easily accessible.

REINCARNATION, *Hinduism & Buddhism*
Souls migrate from body to body, life after life in a spiritual journey to reach enlightenment. Then they become spiritual beings beyond the flesh or are reunited with Brahman, ground of all being.

These seem to be the options. For an immortal soul with an eternity on its hands, there's no logical reason why several of these outcomes couldn't take place or why a loving god couldn't grant a deserving soul its choice, or give it what reward it had come to expect.

Why accept reincarnation?
If the idea of life on Earth being a spiritual journey makes no sense or has no deep appeal for you, then you *won't* accept it. It's as simple as that. If you think it's a test, for example, Christianity or Islam make more sense. Logic won't help. *WITHIN THEIR OWN FRAME OF REFERENCE, ALL THE WORLD'S RELIGIONS MAKE SENSE.* This has to be an intuitive thing. What makes sense for you? Wherever you end up, you will never have earthly proof, nor can anyone dislodge you with facts or logic. All the ancient faiths have had time to sharpen their beliefs to a razor's edge. You pays your money and takes your chances. Having done that, the challenge is to sharpen faith with our best critical judgment. That's what I'm trying to do with my Hindu belief.

Is *Karma* being ground to dust under the Wheel of Life?

That's what it sounds like in much Hindu thought. For many New Agers living good lives in an abundant society, the prospect of being born again sounds just fine. But in India, the idea could easily be more grim.

Consider: you're born. You can't crawl, walk, or speak. You defecate in your pants. So much to learn... you have to go to school... kindergarten and so on, year after year. You work hard to get into a good college... work hard to get into a competitive graduate program and then into a good job. You settle down, have kids... you have to work for them – all your life. Gradually, you start wearing out. You lose your teeth and hair; then your memory. Live long enough and you end up peeing in your pants again and if you can still talk, nobody wants to listen to you anyway.

Then you die... and *poof* you're back into a body again. It's the same old drill. You can't walk or talk. You defecate in your pants. So much to learn! School: kindergarten... first, second, third grade... you get the idea. At some point, it's *not* a New Age adenture any more. You're tired, ground to dust under the Wheel of Life. You want out.

How much more rapidly might you want out if your life was poor, malnourished, and wasted by disease and oppression? Islam and Christianity use Hell to frighten believers into action; Hindus have used life on Earth to do the same thing. "If it's more life you want," says the Hindu, "you've got life after life of it - until you ask for something else."

The prosperity of American life takes some of the sting out of the Hindu vision of Samsara, but prosperity cannot quench our thirst for *meaning*. Here, even to an affluent audience, Hinduism has much to say.

the stages of life:
PLEASURE:
If you love pleasure, enjoy it! Nothing wrong with that; drink your fill of delights. Unlike the Christian and Muslim, Hindus aren't in a hurry. You'll be back.

CONQUEST:
With time, simple hedonism gets dull. There are worlds to conquer, wealth and power to acquire. It's your next step - so go, achieve. You're in the adolescence of your spiritual growth.

SERVICE: (but first, a warning)
Eventually, even victories begin to grow stale. You may be driven to recapture the old thrill of conquest and mastery over nature and over others. As with pleasure, persisting too long without making the next step can lead you into sin or ugliness. Be careful! You are at a place where if you don't go forward, you may lose your way and lose a lot of ground.

Eventually, you see that wealth and power exist only to serve others – so you dedicate yourself to public service. Think of how far you've come. The wheel of life not only revolves, it *rolls*... it makes progress.

WISDOM:
Eventually, though, the inertia of Earth slows you down. The world is so dense and resistant to improvements. Slowly, your attention turns inward. More than anything, you want peace; you want answers about why things are the way they are. Now you're ready for liftoff; you're asking about *enlightenment.*

Is rebirth a punishment or an opportunity? "Neither," says the Hindu. "It's just how it is." serious detours into debauchery, greed, power hunger or cruelty can delay the process for some, but never change the ultimate outcome. In the end, everybody wins.

The problem of life is suffering. The solution to suffering is the search for enlightenment. The reward for enlightenment is union with God. Earth is the school; Karma is the teacher; divinity is the lesson. Some get held back but eventually everybody graduates.

Is pain the only teacher?
I've heard a lot of teachings that picture Karma as cosmic payback, the chickens coming home to roost. If we're punished in this life for the sins of the past one – and if we can't really remember

what we did last time - how can we make progress?

Why should we assume that only pain can teach? That's just not so. If you need to learn compassion, you can learn from example. Someone is kind to you and you decide that that's the way to be - you cultivate kindness. And there you are.

Or... you are an angry, grabby person - and you cling to these vices. At some point, maybe a cosmic calamity may be needed to stun you or simply get your attention. So be it. So was the calamity your Karma? Or was the act of kindness extended to you years before Karma? Was it Karma you should be an eager pupil or that you should be a stubborn one? It was you.

See life as the quest for enlightenment and you seek enlightenment as the reward for every action. You learn to seek no *other* reward. This is hard, to perform every action *for its own sake*... not for praise or honor or thanks, but because each thing was intrinsically worth doing, because it lay in our path on the way to enlightenment.

Karma will keep serving up the lessons. It's not God; it's *us*. What the atheist calls chance the Hindu calls Karma. *Karma is life understood as spiritual opportunity*. Is it cause and effect carried out to its spiritual dimension? That too.

Here's what I think it isn't: *Karma isn't fault.*
The woman who was raped... the Jew in the death
camps... the man dying in a fire... are deserving
objects of our compassion because *they did NOT
create the circumstances of their suffering.* I am
not God. I have no lofty perspective from which
I can observe the suffering of others and
pronounce it their fault. Sometimes, on purely
practical grounds, I can see their own choices
coming back to haunt them, *but not in a Karmic
sense.* If I cannot see clearly what people have
done to cause their own suffering, I have no right
to blame them anyway and assign their pain to
Karma. To the contrary: *the inexplicable pain of
others calls us not to judgment but to compassion
– and to acts of mercy.*

After all, it is to perfect our ability to love that
we are here. We will never understand all the
theology, but we can understand compassion. It
is where, on the practical level, we begin and –
when we lose our bearings – where we begin
again.

WHY WE STRUGGLE WITH THINGS
from the BHAGAVAD - GITA...

Those who lack discrimination may quote the scripture but are really denying its inner truth.

You have the right to work, but for the work's sake only. You have no right to the fruits of work. Desire for the fruits of work must never be your motive for working.

Perform every action with your heart fixed on God. Renounce attachment to the fruits. Be even-tempered in success and failure, for it is this evenness of temper which is meant by yoga.

Work done with anxiety about results is far inferior to work done without such anxiety, in the calm of self-surrender. Seek refuge in the knowledge of Brahman. Those who work selfishly for results are miserable.

To unite the heart with God and then to act: that is the secret...

At present, your mind is bewildered by conflicting interpretations of scripture. When it can rest in contemplation of the in-dwelling soul, THEN you will reach union with God.

What have we said so far?

(A summary of part one)

1) *The idea that the world is made of God, and that we are surrounded by supernatural presence seems to come to Hinduism from humanity's distant past. Not only is Hinduism the world's oldest religion, its organizing principles are far older still.*

2) *Brahman is the central God of Hinduism. Our God does not create the Universe out of nothing: Brahman IS the Universe, and everything in it is made of God.*

3) *We are of God, living in a material world. We love through our egos but are also tempted to feed our egos with power and possessions. So we need help learning how to be here and act like good souls.*

4) *The world is our spiritual school. We return, life after life, to learn our lessons.*

5) *What are our lessons? We are here to love all the forms God can take. That which is God in us must learn to recognize that which is God in everything else - and must learn how to love it.*

6) *We are here to unify soul and substance. We cannot know why God has created the Universe this way, but surely we are here to*

love it and animate it with soul.

7) *Realizing, from a spiritual perspective, what our job is, learning how to do it, and becoming beings that make doing it our central focus, all this is called Enlightenment. It is to achieve enlightenment that we are here.*

8) *There is a system of cause and effect operating at the spiritual level called Karma. It is, from another point of view, our spiritual lesson plan. We cannot expect our lives in Samsara to be easy, but we can at least make them educational. There is some reason to hope that the more seriously we seek wisdom, the less we may have to suffer while learning it.*

9) *We have hope that Brahman, who created this reality, has higher plans for us when we graduate from here. It seems to involve a continued consciousness at a non-physical level. No human being, however full of vision, can really tell us exactly what to expect.*

10) *In the end, we embark on a spiritual path for its own sake – because it is intrinsically worth doing. We are Hindus and Buddhists and Jews and Muslims and Christians because we have chosen to live that way.*

It is precisely because we live our spiritual lives for their own sakes that we do not call religions "certainties"; we call them "faiths".

This is the ancient
Sanscrit symbol for
OM.

It has the same root as
Amen or Amin in Arabic
and serves as a symbol for
Hinduism.

It is also chanted as a tone,
the musical frequency of
the Universe.

PART TWO
PRACTICE
TABLE OF CONTENTS

INTRODUCTION TO PART TWO
- THINGS WE DO -

Most of the world's religions seem to spend more time on telling us what to believe than on how to be. In part, this is because most religions have become *institutions* with priests and buildings to pay for and all the temptations to power that holding the keys to Heaven tempt them with. So getting us to jump through theological hoops has been a historical project for most of the world's major faiths.

What if someone leveled with you and said that people of intelligence and good-will around the globe (and through history) have disagreed profoundly about almost every theological point... so whether Brahman dances on the edge of the Universe or beats in every heart is impossible to pin down. Or whether God's true nature is the Trinity and whether Christ was God in the same way that Krishna was God or that you and I are god is the subject of many opinions *but no certainty*... Can you live with that?

the mystic's path:
If someone said that there is a way you could *feel* God but afterwards, you'd be almost speechless - so you could point to *but not define* the object of your experience... could you live with that? This is the kind of discussion we're headed for.

the Celestial spectrum:
When I was younger, theology fascinated me. I wanted to nail everything down, be *certain* about who God was and how He (God was a guy for me then) worked. I'm still fascinated with all that today, but I'm a lot more relaxed. Now I see all of humanity through all of history feeling in their bones that there is a mind behind nature and that their bodies are haunted by something supernatural. We've been trying to explain it to ourselves for thousands of years and have used all kinds of metaphors and examples and images to do it.

This being the case, you'd think we'd be hungry to know what everyone has come up with. But no. With no material proofs to settle our disagreements, we've turned immediately to coercion and violence. We've been horrible.

the *Two Commandments of God:*
(a reasonable summary of Hindu practice)
What if someone returned from a confrontation with God and said, "I have a message! It's not long, so please pay attention. God has two things to say and two things only:

Look for me.
Be kind.

That's it; that's the message I'm offering you. You could be *anything*, Jew, Muslim, Hindu... anyone could try it! Wouldn't things be better than they are now? If you found God in Heaven and someone else found Brahman in a fallen leaf, you couldn't draw swords over it because you'd have this second commandment - *BE KIND* - to stop you.

Why Hinduism?

I have come to Hinduism because I believe its patient pluralism is the most congenial home for our *Two Commandments*. Hinduism has the fewest built-in temptations to abandon kindness when others disagree - a quality it shares with Buddhism. Besides, I have come to accept the understandings of reincarnation and God's presence in the physical world.

The monotheisms with their one and only one Father-God seem logically imprisoned in an intolerance that seems necessary to them. If there is only one answer and they have it, then everyone else must be wrong. How can they get out of it, even if they want to? So there are lots of gentle people out there with ungentle theologies. And for people intolerant by nature... the monotheisms have a built-in excuse for their intolerance. Just check history.

So what's next?

We're going to take our Two Commandments and discuss how to be a Hindu in America from their perspective. The focus now isn't on theory; it's on *practice*.

We'll be trying to separate Hinduism from Indian culture where we can, because our culture is

Western... we'll be discussing non-violence, because that's basic to Hindu ethics. We'll look into the Hindu view of sex... we'll discuss Hindu concepts on health and healing... we'll discuss how to get communities of Hindus up and running... and we'll close by asking if faith can be globally transformative as well as personally enlightening.

- CHAPTER SIX -

HOW INDIAN DO WE HAVE TO BE ?
(TO BE HINDU)

> *SO ARE PEOPLE GOING TO COME UP TO YOU AND SAY, "FUNNY, YOU DON'T LOOK HINDU..." OR WHAT? NOT TO BE SHALLOW OR ANYTHING, BUT HOW DO YOU 'BE HINDU' IN AMERICA?*

Someone asked the Buddha, "So you gain enlightenment... what do you do next?" Buddha shrugged: "Chop wood?" he suggested. In other words, it is simultaneously true that everything is going to change and nothing is going to change.

What?   When people in India convert to Christianity, do they start dressing up like the *Kilgore Rangerettes* from a football halftime? If you like fashions from India, or the music (there's some *fabulous* trance and global music available) go for it, but that's got nothing to do with faith.

Consider the inverse: how much unchristian behavior has been offered up by people in clerical garb over the years? Spiritually speaking, clothes maketh *not* the man. So don't worry about it. Hardly anyone knows I'm Hindu and those I tell think I must be at least half kidding. Nothing wrong with that.

If there's one outward manifestation of Hinduism (and Buddhism) I'd recommend to you, it's the *"Namaste"* gesture one makes upon meeting and parting. It means *"I honor the God within you."* The hands are pressed together over the heart and one makes a little bow. When it's extra heartfelt, sometimes the hands stay pressed and the fingertips touch the heart and then lightly touch the forehead. I'm sure in India, routine business probably makes this a perfunctory gesture much of the time, but for Westerners who are new to it, perhaps this salute from soul to soul can be made more consciously. So it may only be done from time to time, but when you feel it, make it — meaning by it *Namaste,* (Naa - maa - *stay*) I honor the God within you. It's a sweet thing to do.

When my mother was dying of cancer, I had explained what Namaste meant and when we parted, she said goodby that way. I cannot tell you how much it means when it's really meant.

One of the weaknesses of the New Age movement is how much money has found its way into it. This is not charity money, set aside by believers for the sake of others, it's *marketing* money. Apparently, when you become interested in Shamanistic practices, Wicca or Eastern religions, a lot of people are counting on you buying all this stuff. If you need that to stay mindful of what you're about, then fine. Why not? But Hinduism isn't a fashion statement, especially in India.

The Hindu gods are depicted in Hindu art and sculpture dressed as they are because royalty dressed that way in India long before the birth of Christ. The music and sculpture was simply the natural expression of that culture. Should we then conclude that God wears ankle bracelets and sandals and thinks in Sanscrit (or Hebrew or Latin?) Borrow what you like, but it's got nothing to do with Hinduism in America. For us, born in America to overwhelmingly Christian and Jewish families, adopting Hinduism means adopting Hindu *concepts* and *practice*. This shouldn't cost you a dime. Millions of wonderful Hindus in India barely have a dime, and it doesn't slow them up.

Instead, we should be looking at something Hindu that really counts for something: the principle of *non-violence*.

- CHAPTER SEVEN -

Non-Violence

> The principle of non-violence is so basic to
> Hinduism that we must start any discussion of
> Hindu practice here.

Gandhi's gift:

Mahatma Gandhi is perhaps the most beloved
Hindu known in the West. In his life, in his
political action, he mobilized the idealism latent in
his people and directed it against the English. At
the same time, he reminded the English of their
own idealism and made them ashamed of their
greed and brutality. In this way, he freed his
country from colonial rule with remarkably little
bloodshed.

So what?

Did the English remain morally transformed by
their experience with Gandhi? Not on your life!
Nor were the Indian people innoculated against
their own shortcomings. What both British and
Indians were left with - what we *all* were left with
- was a vision of how ordinary people could be
transformed by spiritual power. If you are
involved in any kind of personal spiritual search,
please hold out for nothing less than
transformation. Expect to remain your normal
self... yet somehow capable of transcending that

normal self.

the place to start:
We can resolve that whatever short-comings we suffer from, we can refrain from hitting people. *We can refrain from hitting people.* It's that simple. We can get angry, *really* angry, but when we feel that anger about to translate itself into some kind of physical action, we can jump on ourselves and wrestle that violent impulse to the ground. We *have* to.

the moral minimum:
That is the first step to a non-violent life - that no one is actually struck, no physical pain, no violence will come from us. No one should be close to us because they are afraid to run away. People should seek our company because they know that no harm will come from us.

There is, particularly for men, the attraction of danger. We project the aura of danger, that we are men to be reckoned with. Don't mess with us. As Hindus, we reject that message and the power over others that violence and the threat of violence might give us.

harmlessness:
We are not egos let loose in the world; we are souls given bodies to better love the world on the world's terms. We are not harmless because we are cowards; we are harmless because we remember what we are, and we reject power over others as a pleasure counter to our spiritual best

interest.

Here is a general kind of rule that has exceptions but is generally true: *if we make someone cry, we have probably done something wrong.* Even with children who need discipline, we should have some misgivings when we make *them* cry too.

In *every* case, we try to control our anger first. Then when we have ourselves under control, we can share the causes of our anger with others. The bottom line is that *we do no harm.*

All this can be very difficult, almost unimaginably so for some people. But we have to try.

Harmlessness is the basis of all morality.

---

in what we say...
Then we can observe our speech. How can we speak so that no one is offended or wounded? This is also difficult, but vital. You see, in the process of becoming harmless in speech and action, we transform ourselves into people from whom only good things come. Do you have any idea how the world aches for people like that? In the Path of Compassion, we seek to become that which the world needs.

In the beginning, progress may seem slow and uncertain, but keep working on it. Slowly, living this way will become automatic - just an expression of who you are. That is the goal.

Any exceptions?
There have been times when men and women have been forced to defend themselves. One cannot expect *sacrificial* non-violence from everyone. What we can ask is that whenever we use force - even in self-defense - we respond to it with regret. I'm reminded of the Gulf War and the joy and amusement so many people took from the videotapes of smart bombs dropping down the smokestacks of Iraqi buildings. We should always regret the loss of life - *all* life. If violence becomes entertainment for us, we'll shrivel up spiritually and become our own casualties.

Hindus stand at the opposite end of the spectrum from fundamentalist extremists who claim God gave them licenses to kill. God has not told us to kill; God has told us to *heal*. Every scripture has told us this. There is no land, no wealth, no dignity, no entitlement, no insult nor injury for which God has written humanity a blank check redeemable in someone's tears and blood. To the contrary: we are commanded to love, compassion, and forgiveness.

So non-violence is our first practice and the most indispensable. It is, in positive terms, *PATIENCE* - the acceptance that the world moves according to its own designs. The opposite of violence is not just its absence; it's *patience*. It's a positive attitude we take when things get frustrating: bemusement... relaxation... acceptance. We warp our spiritual reality out of shape by insisting the world always conform to our wishes.

Of course we'll slip up, but we can catch ourselves before things get too far. And *absolutely*, no one gets hurt.

"Hell has three doors," says the Bhagavad-Gita, *lust, rage, and greed. These lead to our ruin; therefore we must avoid them all."* Seen a different way, there is another opposite to violence: *REVERENCE*. To harm anyone is to forget that God is within them. Forget God and we've forgotten everything.

ON COMPASSION, *from the BHAGAVAD - GITA:*

The Lord lives in the heart of every creature.

Who burns with the bliss and suffers the sorrow of every creature within their own heart, making their own each bliss and each sorrow: THOSE I hold highest of all the yogis.

- CHAPTER EIGHT -

WHAT ABOUT SEX ?

Christianity seems to have such a conflicted position on this (what with Saint Paul and most of the other church fathers) that it's natural for an American to ask what Hinduism thinks of sex.

It has mixed feelings.

giving it up:
For those on the Path of Renunciation, sex is a problem. From the perspective of Renunciation, physical sensations reinforce the illusion that the flesh is real - or to put it another way, the intensity of our sensations tends to blind us to our spiritual natures. Since for intensity you just can't beat sex, the Path of Renunciation gives it a wide berth.

What is it about sex that so many religions want us to do without it or - failing that - spoil our enjoyment of it?

I suspect the status of women has a lot to do with it. Ancient historians reported that the Goddess religions were downright *"orgiastic"*, as several of them put it. So when women had status and when God was a woman, sex was good. When women fell in men's esteem, men still wanted sex but now they had to ahem and excuse me about it as though everyone knew they'd be better off if they could give it up. Like smoking. The saints said giving it up was easy; they'd done it thousands of times.

making it sacred:
What's so sweet about Hinduism is that it offers multiple paths to almost everything. So Hinduism says, "OK, you can't give up sex - or you don't want to... there's *another* path to enlightenment that not only doesn't detour around sex, *it runs right through it!* It's called *TANTRIC* sex. If Hindus can't give it up, they make it a science.

"I am the beginning, the middle, and the end of Creation," says Krishna in the Bhagavad-Gita. *"I am the essence of the waters, the shining of the sun and the moon, the Om in all the Vedas, the word that is God. I am the sacred smell of the Earth, light of the fire, Life of all lives."* Your lover is God - because *everything* is made of God.

So how do Hindus approach sex? Worshipfully. Even as a pure pleasure, the Path of Renunciation is comfortable offering you sex manuals *(the Kama Sutra)* knowing that the sooner you satiate yourself, the sooner you'll look for deeper things. Meanwhile, the Tantric Path wants to get your chakras (spiritual "organs") involved so when you make love, you'll feel a more perfect union with your lover. If your orgasms are more intense, more frequent, and longer-lasting, so much the better. Who ever told us *souls* couldn't come? There are numerous books available that explain Tantric sex in patient detail, should this interest you.

more invisible changes:
Here we go again: we're revisiting the idea that we can do the same things we always did - and yet everything can be different. See the world as Samsara and it *is* Samsara. See the world as filled up with souls in body suits and you'll Namaste each one - and, when you make love, it will be soul to soul. Of course, you'll be using your body to do it, but then your body will be an instrument in the hands of your lover's soul. When it's really not the same as it used to be, you'll know you've gotten somewhere.

> *Spiritual sex is not a matter of technique. It's a matter of APPROACH.*

We have *Namaste* for everyone we meet in our life on Earth. We have sex to not only honor but *caress* the soul of the partner we've been given in this life. To *that*, Hinduism says AMEN!

ON MARRIAGE, *the Yajur Veda & the Upanishads:*

Oh man and woman.... proclaim your intention to enter the married life... observing the noble virtue of non-violence, and uplift your soul. Converse together happily, living in a peaceful home. Spoil not your life.

In truth, it is not for the love of a husband that a husband is dear, but for the love of the SOUL in the husband that the husband is dear. It is not for the love of a wife that a wife is dear, but for the love of the SOUL in the wife that the wife is dear.

As someone in the arms of one beloved feels only peace all around, even so the soul in the embrace of God feels only peace all around. But in the ocean of Spirit, the seer is alone, beholding his own immensity. This is the world of Brahman... this is the supreme joy.

On a portion of that joy, all other beings live.

- CHAPTER NINE -

HEALTH
AND HEALING

---

*There are ancient Indian traditions of healing
that have attracted interest in the West, but
some are more cultural than spiritual. Hindu
approaches to health and healing seem to be
grounded in principles of compassion for all
sentient creatures or in visions of ourselves as
spiritual beings. Let's briefly look at diet,
healing and meditation from these
perspectives.*

Must we be vegetarians?
Since ancient times, the cow has been sacred in
India and protected. It's hard for us to
understand, in the age of the *Big Mac* how little
meat figures into the diet of poor people. A cow
that gave milk to drink and turn into butter and
cheese, and dropped dung that could be burned as
fuel was the gift that kept on giving. Poor people
weren't foolish enough to slaughter it so they
could eat for only a week. There's nothing
particularly spiritual about this, but it must have
been a factor in the beginning of a reverence for
life.

Then too, we have evidence that the cow (and/or the bull) was sacred in the Indus Valley civilizations in 2,500 BC. when Hinduism was beginning. During this historical period, the sun was rising in the constellation Taurus the Bull at the Spring equinox. In the procession of the equinoxes, each constellation gets about 2,200 years in this spot and ancient societies seem to have encorporated the astral symbols of their age into their religion and art.

Pisces had just begun to swing into place at the time of Christ and early Christians used the fish symbol as shorthand for their new age. For ancient India (and for their Minoan contemporaries) the bull was the central symbol. In the Mediterranean basin, bulls were ceremonially sacrificed; in India they were ceremonially spared. (There are alternatives to sacrificing the sacred.)

The idea of vegetarianism is rooted in reincarnation. Buddha would explain that the soul of any animal could be your own departed mother, for all you knew. That was a dramatic way of driving home the principle that the divinity in all creatures was essentially the same. Human consciousness is what souls in human bodies get, but the spirit that animates all life is always God. What should direct our discussion is not concern about whether another creature can think but whether it can *suffer*.

If you are going to eat meat, you might inquire into the conditions under which the animals we consume live out their lives and under which they are killed. By these lights, we should prefer free-range animals that at least have a *life* before their death.

As a second, more difficult step, we can prefer protein from the *least* sentient level of animal possible, preferring fowl to mammals and preferring fish to fowl. It is generally thought that suffering increases with sentience.

Thirdly, we can simply reduce our meat intake across the board - have several meatless nights a week, for example. From a pure health perspective, what we've said so far represents sound cardiovascular advice anyway.

We can combine rice and red beans to make excellent protein that's more easily broken down in the body than meat. So we can actually live nice fat-free lives and never eat meat at all, if that's our conviction. There's a lot of literature available in health-food stores about *macrobiotic* diets and other approaches to vegetarian living if this interests you. I think it's fair to say that Hinduism expects us to be interested.

a spiritual vision of the body:
It is a notion found in ancient China and India in that the body has currents and focal-points of *energy* which have a profound role in health and healing. For the Chinese, there is *KI* or *CHI*,

rivers of energy moving through the body. From India, we get the idea of *CHAKRAS*, energy centers located along the body's centerline. *("...like buttons on a clown suit," as one of my students put it.)*

Chakra means "wheel" in Sanscrit. In Hindu understanding, there is a chakra at the crown of the head, at mid-forehead, throat, heart, solar plexus, navel, and groin. These seem to correspond to specific endocrine glands and are simultaneously rooted in various qualities and powers of the spirit. So the chakras might be thought of as access points to where the body and soul communicate. This sounds far-fetched, but the healing system of *REIKI* is based on this approach and (like accupuncture works with *CHI*) *REIKI* seems to work too. Sometimes you get actual healing; more often you get relief from pain. Sometimes too, you see people fall deeply asleep and snore, then wake up and discuss something that deeply hurt them – like a childhood trauma. I am married to a Reiki Master and have experienced and witnessed the power of this kind of healing.

In nursing, a less spiritual approach to the same technique is called *therapeutic touch*. This is something you can learn, as well as read about. As you experience giving it or receiving it, you are quite literally practicing your faith. In yet another variation of *tantra* and *namaste*, your soul interacts with another. Here it isn't exactly greeting or caressing; it is *healing*. This too is love in motion, which is what spiritual practice is all about.

what it's like:
Here, I can only speak of my own experience. For others, it's probably different. Practicing Reiki is a bit like listening through your hands. It has that kind of quality to it – of straining to hear an elusive sound. When someone is hurt somewhere, you place the hands just above the place and meditate there. When things work best for me, I feel a heat growing in the space under my hands. Then I lower my hands gently onto the spot and do two things at once: I send that warmth to the pain and *I listen through my hands* for it. Sometimes, there is a sense of pulsing energy or of tiny bubbles popping. The object is to get the pain to dissolve, flow away, be exhaled with the person's breath. I may suggest that last one: to breathe out the pain and let go of it. If we don't want to hurt, to try letting go of the pain and the fear of pain... breathe it out... replace it with light and warmth under the skin. Energy flows through the crowns of our heads and through our hands into the one who's hurting. Not from us but *through* us. Where does this energy come from? Because I'm a Hindu, I believe it's from Brahman... from God.

To Western medicine, grounded in the scientific method, this is rubbish. Your *intention* to relieve pain, all by itself, means nothing to science and it's considered magical thinking to assume that thoughts or intentions have power of their own... but that is exactly what the healing traditions of almost every faith insist on. In spiritual matters, everything hinges on intention. Anyone can lay hands on someone, but the intention to heal, the intention to direct love like a searchlight, is something else. That intention can be casual – or better, it can be the product of disciplined training and concentration. It can be a form of prayer. Those who send and receive it have experienced its power. There are excellent books – and people to train with – for anyone wanting to pursue this further.

meditation:
Recent cardiac research demonstrates an interesting fact: *meditation is good for you.* It lowers heart-rate and blood pressure. There is some evidence that cancer patients have helped reduce tumors by visualizing their destruction. One patient visualized his T cells as beautiful white husky dogs attacking a multi-tentacled monster.

Western medicine is reluctantly coming round to the realization that spiritual practice positively influences health, though that wouldn't surprise a Hindu – or a Christian, for that matter. (Actually, it may be the *insurance* companies that endorse this first. Spiritual healing is a lot cheaper than medical healing.) Slowly, we might grow into a happy synthesis of spirit and science in which the powers of both combine, rather than compete.

yoga:
The Indo-European word *yoga* has the same root as the word *yoke*. In its most familiar Western form, it's a discipline of flexing, body positions and breathing – often combined with techniques of meditation – to condition the body for health and the reception of insight. Since Hinduism sees things pluralistically, it offers many kinds of yoga paths – some steep, some mild – for us to follow. Your local health club or YMCA probably has at least one program in yoga – and you can check the bulletin board of your health-food store for more spiritually ambitious programs. Again, there's a lot of literature available on this.

some ideas:
Remember our Two Commandments of God: *Look for Me... be kind?* We can apply both to our practices of health and healing.

Vegetarians can see God in their fellow creatures and – out of kindness and reverance – decline to eat them.

In Reiki, we can look for the spiritual in our bodies and in the bodies of others. Also, we look for the hurt – and send light and love for healing.

We talked about meditation in chapter 4. You can try to find 15 minutes a day. Do you get relaxed in the shower? Why not place your hands over each chakra one at a time and tone a nice deep OM for two breaths on each. Close your eyes and visualize light and warmth soaking into you at each station. Meanwhile, *purify your intentions at each chakra:* to keep an open channel to God... to listen continually to your inner voice... to speak kindly and honestly all day... to see everyone you deal with as embodied souls... to restrain your appetite for power over others... to restrain your appetites in general... to keep your sexual energy to yourself until you share it lovingly with your partner. From crown to groin, you have a purification for each chakra.

Let the water run off your hands between each one... gather a breath and begin the next. Soak in the light. End in a namaste: hands like a steeple before your heart. Honor the God within yourself. Maybe your family thinks it's weird at first. So what? Square up to live your day as a god-centered person. Touch your steepled fingers to your forehead before you let go. Amen.

You can meditate while sailing or playing a musical instrument or dancing or watching images emerge in a darkroom tray. You can even learn to *write* in meditation. Open yourself to the voice within you and let language flow onto the page without prior consideration or self-censorship. You can practice these things so long as you can remain pointed in your *intention* to transform mundane activity into a form of worship or to open yourself to an awareness of God. As Hindu scriptures put it, *"Keep God spinning in the midst of all your activities."* It is a recurring theme here that *intention* is at the heart of spiritual practice.

for the world:
From a Tibetan Lama I learned another kind of meditation - one for the benefit of others:

Get settled and quiet. Focus on your breathing until the buzz of interior chatter is at least manageable. Think of anyone you know or have ever known who has been unhappy or in pain... Visualize the teeming streets of a city and imagine how many of those who walk before you are unhappy or in pain. Now you drive through the suburbs at night and see all the lighted windows blur past; you lift off and see city after city. The evening news reminds you that 100 wars smolder all around the world. *Breathe out white light to everyone everywhere in compassion for their suffering.*

When you inhale, *imagine you're breathing in darkness* - taking the suffering of the world into yourself. Light out... darkness in... healing out... suffering in... Are you going to make yourself sick this way? No. Your *soul* can do what your body can't: take in toxins and return nutrients. Pain in, love out. Make regular time for this. While it uses the techniques of meditation, it's really a kind of prayer.

"Come on, " you say, "this is magic! You don't *really* think this kind of mumbo-jumbo is going to change anything, do you? Do you?"

Prove it doesn't. Besides, this I know: develop an active and compassionate prayer life... be kind, look for God... and certainly *YOU* are changed. Science is never going to confirm spiritual intervention because it's situational, non-repeatable. The stories about it will be circumstantial, anecdotal - inadmissable as evidence. So what? Do you want a scientific materialism to run your life? Ask the sceptic that.

It is historical and scientific to believe that pain and suffering are passed in a horrible inheritance from generation to generation. We've read history; we've all seen it. It is spiritual to believe that suffering can be inhaled into the heart and *absorbed* and *destroyed* there - and only forgiveness comes out. We've seen this too. If that is what we want, we know what to do.

We're getting near the end of our discussion.

What have we said about being a Hindu so far?

1) We've offered the Two Commandments of God as a summary of Hindu practice:
   "LOOK FOR ME..." and "BE KIND."

2) Hinduism in America won't look particularly Indian. You'll be an exceptionally kind American who understands God differently than most of the neighbors.

3) *An American Hindu will embrace the principle of non-violence and put it into practice in speech as well as action.*

4) *If you are not sexually active, Hinduism offers a way to use celibacy as part of your spiritual growth. If you enjoy sex, Hinduism suggests you investigate a more spiritual sexuality to reverence the god in your partner. That there is more pleasure in it is a happy bonus.*

5) *Because Hindus believe the same spirit lives in all creatures, the suffering and needless death of animals is a problem. For many Hindus, being vegetarian is an appropriate response.*

6) *Hindus seek God in each other and practice meditation and healing techniques that offer spiritual comfort for others. It's a way of looking for God and being kind at the same time.*

These are all things Hindus can do on their own. Next, we need to imagine what we might do in groups.

ON MEDITATION, *from the BHAGAVAD - GITA*

The place where we sit should be firm, situated on a clean spot. As we sit there, we are to hold the senses and imagination in check and keep the mind concentrated upon its object.

Our posture should be motionless, with the head and neck held erect, and the vision indrawn... not looking about.

Yogi is not for overeaters nor for those who fast excessively. It is not for those who sleep too much, nor for the keeper of exaggerated vigils. Let us be moderate in our eating and recreation, moderately active, moderate in sleep and in wakefulness.

If we practice meditation in this manner, our hearts will become pure... and our minds under control. A flame does not flicker in a wind-less place.

Yogis see God in all things and all things in God. They never lose sight of God, nor does God lose sight of them.

- CHAPTER TEN -

MAKING A RELIGION

> There are Hindu things we could do on a
> desert island. Being solitary Hindus in a sea
> of Christians would be a lot like that. What
> could a whole bunch of us do and what would
> that be like?

Consider Hinduism in India:
In India there are almost a billion Hindus. For
them, Hinduism is a broad river like the Ganges.
You're born in the river and flow in it all your
life. Your birth, marriage, death, all take place in
a Hindu context. Hymns, daily prayers, gods
preferred by your family and village, the way you
imagine those gods... are part of your intellectual
furniture. It's the same for people born in *any*
faith when the whole society is flowing with you,
bearing you up, and sweeping you along.

If you've been reading this book and thinking that
maybe you've *always* been a Hindu but never
realized it, you don't have the current with you.
You're not only alone, you must swim against the
cultural stream in which you were born - or at
least *across* it. You need company.

Much of the energy of religion is collective.
Religion is *social* for most of the world's people.
Consider a honey bee. Trap just one and it will

hum in its bottle for you. *"OMmmm..."* It will have all the genetic information honey bees have – but that's it. Now get a whole *bunch* of honey bees together and they will suddenly go to work throwing up temples and storehouses and nurseries. The whole bee thing only happens with groups. That's when the honey gets made.

(That's when the *mischief* gets made too, but we're going to try to avoid doing any of that.)

We need to find each other.
How can we do that? Internet would be a good field to search in. Post an invitation; search. You could run a newspaper ad for a discussion group on Eastern religion. Lonesome Buddhists might show up, which would be fine. They're first cousins. Although Buddhism avoids discussing God, you have a lot in common. New Age people might come out of hunger or curiosity. Hinduism is pluralistic, so you can welcome everybody.

You can contact organizations, too. (Several are listed at the end of the book.) They can be a useful source of books as well as guidance and company.

You can contact local bookstores and propose a discussion night based on texts of Eastern religions. You might draw up a short list with the manager and make sure several of each are in stock. Many bookstores *love* this kind of activity.

See if local talk radio or community-access TV would be interested in programming that might spread the word that you're out there. When I've taught evening adult courses in World Religion, Hinduism has drawn the most interest and people have, half kidding (but only half), asked about forming a church. Over and over, I've heard people say they realized they'd been Hindu all along and not known it.

What can you all do?
You can begin by studying Hinduism together. Make up a discussion group. Read different texts and scriptures and teach each other what you've gotten from them; read favorite passages aloud.

The reading aloud part will be your first step towards getting some form of worship service started. At each point, you can discuss what you actually want out of this.

Who is worshipped?
I have imagined that the pantheon of Hindu gods will be of intellectual interest but will probably not make sense to most Americans *as objects of worship*. The God of gods in Hinduism has various aspects who are understood to be one, yet are named according to their function or according to the aspect of reality they represent. *BRAHMAN* is the God of gods - beyond imagining. God *as creator* is BRAHMA, spelled without the *N*. God the *preserver* of reality is VISHNU and god the Destroyer who recycles reality - absorbing it back

into the Divine – is SHIVA. But they're all God.
How you want to handle this and whether you'll
simply use the name of God but mean Hindu
things by it... you'll want to discuss this and find
something workable.

making your own channel:
You won't have a river of faith to flow with.
You'll have to start off as a modest trickle and
create your own channel as you grow. That's
how every faith has done it at the beginning.
Theology gets refined, prayers get written.
Decisions get made on whether to have rituals and
what kinds and how much. It starts with a core
of experience and belief, but ordinary people
always made the decisions on where to take it.
You'll do that too.

meditation:
Most Buddhist groups I'm familiar with meet
principally for meditation. On one hand,
meditation seems like a solitary activity, but there
is strength in numbers and opportunity for people
to discuss what they've been experiencing.
Groups make the OM chant much more powerful
and moving. You should try it.

The Society of Friends (Quakers) have been doing
group meditation for years. They maintain silence
until someone is moved to speak. More silent
reflection follows, more shared thoughts and so
on till the meeting ends and they all go home.

Meditation is such a basic part of Hindu practice, I'd imagine you'd want to devote time to it in group meetings. Meditation for others as described in the chapter on health and healing makes sense for group worship.

The practice of Reiki and other forms of meditative healing makes sense too and would create a wholly different kind of experience - less cerebral and more nurturing.

acts of compassion:
Many Hindus and Buddhists in the East have charitable intentions but no financial resources to do much charitable work. Prayers are all they can offer. Hindus in America are likely to have more financial ability to do public good. Communities of faith can see what their neighborhoods need and can organize some help - or can offer to assist some larger church (any denomination) in a worthy project

All these things and more that you might think up, mixed in whatever proportions as seem reasonable, can be part of the community life of American Hinduism.

spiritual pluralism:
Such an approach as we're discussing here leads to a wide variety of practice and belief. It is linked to a common core, but there is tremendous latitude - and that latitude is typically Hindu. In India, that latitude has its traditional variety of expression and in America, we'll have ours. That

seems right and necessary.

relations with other faiths:

These should always be cordial. Conversations with Buddhists will be especially beneficial because Buddhism places so much emphasis on clear thinking. It's *always* good for us to swap ideas with clear thinkers - and, like us, Buddhists rarely get hot under the collar or turn every conversation into an attempted conversion.

New Age people probably also share common beliefs in non-violence, reincarnation, and spiritual healing. Hinduism may offer them a more developed concept of God and a connection to a world-wide faith.

With Christians and others, things may get more dicey. Monotheisms are logically structured to accept one truth and, once having it, exclude all other possibilities. "How," they ask, "can two contradictory propositions *both* be true?"

Arguments make no sense. We can only urge humility on two grounds:

1) There is no external authority to which *all* faiths will willingly yield to resolve our disagreements. In the absence of such an authority, it is reasonable for us to be tolerant.

2) Operating with such limited mental equipment, we would be arrogant to claim adequate understanding of who God is and how the

universe manages its affairs. *Humility* seems to be the first appropriate response to a belief in God.

If Christians or anyone just can't talk to you without trying to convert you, then gracefully withdraw. Tell them they have an ancient and beautiful faith and that you'd feel just awful if they gave it up on your account...

Anyone who can discuss theology cheerfully and with genuine curiosity is a gem. You will learn a lot and clarify your own mind in their company.

All religions as they grow are tempted to abuse whatever wealth and institutional power they get their hands on. Smaller groups are vulnerable to little power plays, rigidity, and acts of petty snobbery. Hinduism in India is local and decentralized. Small problems have nowhere to go. American Hinduism would be lucky to enjoy 4,500 more years of such charming tolerance. Let's work on it.

from the *BRIHAD-ARANYAKA UPANISHAD*

> *It is not for the love of religion that religion is dear, but for the love of the SOUL in religion that religion is dear.*

CONCLUSION

- GANDHI'S PATH -

the nice Assyrian:
Around 900 B.C. along the Tigris river, there lived a militaristic society called the Assyrians. They were the terror of the ancient world, not only conquering city after city but raping, pillaging, and even skinning whole populations alive and leaving pyramids of stacked skulls and smouldering mounds of flesh behind them.

And yet we can imagine there must have been nice Assyrians... the noble priestess trying to maintain the dignity of Innunu and the status of women in general... the honest grocer... the sweet and gentle whore. They were kind and generous people. By the understanding of their religion, *they were good people.* None the less, the rape and brutality of their civilization continued – despite their personal qualities.

So it is with us.
There's nothing globally transformative about being a nice person. Whatever the reigning faith, the caste system, slavery, inquisition and exploitation have rolled on in every society. In the absence of a conscious effort to change the terms under which we all live our lives, being virtuous is exactly like being a priest on the Titanic. We're kind... we're a comfort... we're doomed.

Aren't we all doomed anyway? Of course we are. But why should anyone have to go third class? Why can't we lift our vision and imagine a life transformed by love, gentleness, and generosity? What is the difference between a life softened by these qualities and a life *transformed* by them? I believe the difference is INTENTION.

Gandhi's path:

Gandhi was a Hindu and I'm borrowing from his life and teaching. He was not content to practice his personal virtues under a general condition of injustice and opression. He intended to transform the fundamental system under which the Britsh and his fellow Indians lived out their lives. He intended a transformation of life into something more grounded in the actual values of Hinduism and less grounded in fear and greed. There have been precious few human beings of any age with the courage of convictions like these – and he's considered a saint: *Mahatma...* "great soul." So of the many paths Hinduism offers, I'd like to add one last one: the path of Gandhi – *The Path of Transformation.*

practicing faith for the *world's* sake:

By believing in God and the soul within us, we have already accepted a proposition more fantastic than any utopia. It will take great discipline to act socially and politically without seeking the traditional rewards of wealth and power that accomplishment offers. Can we, like Gandhi, intend not just social improvement but social *transformation?* Can working for that be a Hindu path?

I'm trying not to preach or lean on you too hard here because I am not Gandhi and I have no right to lay any guilt on you if you aren't either. But he *did* blaze a path, and history reminds us that thousands of people followed it. It was a Hindu path and as I finish writing this, I'm realizing that it's what I want to leave you with more than anything.

If we follow the Path of Transformation, we will probably have to accept that at the end of our lives, we may be unable to see the fruits of our efforts. Still, we'll be able to say that it was enlightening - which is, after all, what we've been seeking.

Maybe if you try to be kind to everyone in your reach, that will be more than enough. Surely enough people living gently and justly will change the way life feels for everyone - and I would be overjoyed if more people did that. But if we were bold enough to ask for even more, maybe we would get it. Maybe we'll never get it *UNLESS* we ask for it. Knowing what to ask for in specific terms will take enormous thought, but we can each begin somewhere.

So now I'm asking you one final question: Will you take the path of Gandhi and be in the world to save the world? Will you try to do this humbly, remembering how humanity tends to subvert even its best intentions? Will you do this faithfully, knowing how the world resists improvement? Will you do this cheerfully, knowing that living your highest nature cannot fail to reward you with enlightenment? I know that you need enlightenment but the world itself needs *light*. Will you try to be a light for the world?

I promise you that if you do, God will put a lamp in your hand.

PRINCIPLES OF HINDUISM

---

1) *Everything in the Universe is made of God.*

2) *Therefore everything in nature is sacred. We see truly when we see the God in everything.*

3) *We experience the divine best when it is close to us. When we do, it seems that God is in many forms. But in a larger sense, we know that God is One – the God of Gods.*

4) *We believe that existence is cyclical, issuing out from God (Brahman), changing form and evolving spiritually, and eventually returning to its source. We call this reincarnation.*

5) *There is no way we're going to really under-stand any of this, but we believe we are here to experience the world, learn from it, and to simultaneously recognize the divinity in it and in ourselves.*

6) *Our spiritual lesson-plan, the circumstances under which we learn it – and the consequences of our failure to learn it – are called KARMA.*

7) *Understanding our divinity and living harmoniously with that understanding is called ENLIGHTENMENT. Whether enlightenment requires absolute perfection, whatever claims seers and savants might make, is known only to God. We seek enlightenment for its own sake, as the happiest and richest way to be.*

8) *For those of us in the West, we may need to separate our understanding of Hinduism from the cultural patterns of India so that it can live for us here as it does in India for believers there.*

9) *The first and most obvious expression of our belief is non-violence, reverence for life, in our actions and in our speech.*

10) *We need a regular rhythm of prayer and meditation to become aware of God's presence. Here, Hindu tradition has many useful pointers.*

11) *We have a spiritual obligation to assist others in their suffering and to find remedies for the causes of their suffering. We pray for those whom we cannot personally assist and practice spiritual healing also.*

12) *We recognize that Hinduism offers multiple paths for people of different temperaments and at different stages in their lives. This neither a rigid nor a hierarchical faith.*

13) *We consider our faith and greet the faiths of others in humility, knowing that no one can really claim knowledge of God's nature or of God's plans for the Universe. All our best thinking and the language we use to explain it only points to reality beyond our understanding and motivates us to seek God in ourselves and in everything around us.*

14) *The Two Commandments of God are: LOOK FOR ME and BE KIND. Use these as points of reference when lost or confused.*

APPENDIX – 1
SOME USEFUL READING

This book isn't intended to be a one-source encyclopedia on Hinduism. If you're interested in all this, there are two kinds of sources to investigate: SCRIPTURES and COMMENTARIES about Hindu belief and practice. I'm going to list some books that have been helpful to me, knowing that there are many more for you to discover on your own. This is just a start.

SCRIPTURES:

The Hindu scriptures are the oldest in the world. The VEDAS are the oldest of these. They're a rich source of prayers and a good look at the developing theology of India. Later scriptures offer a more complete understanding of Hinduism as it evolved.

<u>THE UPANISHADS</u>   These are collections of writings by various Hindu thinkers. Points of view and focus vary. You'll find everything from prayers to stories here. Published collections will draw on different writings; there are far more Upanishads than most bookstore texts include. I've used the PENGUIN edition and admired its opening commentary.

<u>THE BHAGAVAD-GITA</u> (The Song of God)
This scripture could be part of the Upanishads, but it's so useful and well-loved that it appears on its own as a summary of Hinduism's central beliefs. Gandhi kept one by his bedside most of his life. The *MENTOR* edition has a priceless introduction by Aldous Huxley that is alone worth the price of the book.

COMMENTARIES:

These range from writings by Indian Hindus to Western descriptions of Hindu belief and practice to a Christian critique.

<u>AUTOBIOGRAPHY OF A YOGI</u> by Swami Paramahansa Yogananda, *SELF-REALIZATION FELLOWSHIP PUBLICATIONS*. This book has been hugely successful for decades and has given several generations a mental picture of Hindu life and its possibilities. This is an extradordiny tale told in a modest voice. Its central point is that *matter is obedient to spirit.* Miraculous events abound, along with descriptions of the yogi's path to mastery of one's self and of the material world. This is a good counterpoint to all the analytical discussions of Hindu theology. You'll have to decide whether you agree with the yogi's fundamental thesis - or not. Your answer will largely determine what sort of a Hindu you'll be, or if you'll want to be one at all.

THE BOOK OF GANDHI WISDOM by Trudy S. Settel, Citidel Press. This is a small, compact collections of Gandhi's thoughts on a variety of topics. If you want to do more than scratch the surface of his life and thinking, there is also the story of his life and much more. Here is a man who combined the Path of Renunciation with a career of political and social activism – and got stunning results.

World Faiths – HINDUISM by Kanitar & Cole, NTC Books offers a vivid portrait of the daily life and practice of Hindoos today – both in India and in the West. There are some useful discussions of belief but, most helpful are the detailed explanations of Hinduism as it is practiced in home and temple within its culture of origin. Without intending to, the book makes a good case for why Westerners will need to reinvent much of Hinduism's devotional practices, while hanging on to the theological heart of the faith. The actual purpose of the book seems to be assisting residents of Britain in understanding the growing numbers of Hindus in their midst.

A POPULAR DICTIONARY OF HINDUISM by Kavel & Werner, NTC Books begins with a lucid discussion of Hinduism then, in alphabetical order, explains concepts, important thinkers divinities and sacred events. A *very* useful book.

APOLOGETICS IN THE NEW AGE - a Christian
critique of pantheism by Clark & Geisler, Baker
Book House, Grand Rapids, Michigan. Most
Christian approaches to other theologies seem to
consist of matching alternative ideas to quotations
from Christian scripture, pointing out the
discrepancies, and thus rejecting the alternative
view as un-Christian. This volume is far less
simple-minded, more respectful and much more
rigorous. It *does* seek to challenge pantheism -
the belief that God is present *within* creation, that
the world is made of God. In the process, the
book offers an excellent historical view of who
has offered Pantheism to the world and how
they've done it. It teaches Pantheism quite well.
I think its critique fails on several fronts. In
criticizing the mystic's preference of experience
over reason, the book turns its back on the
Christian mystics, Jesus among them, who
breathed the breath of life into the faith - and on
the many personal experiences of grace that give
believers their reason to believe. In its only real
short-cut, the book pretends that pantheists
imagine that *all* of the Divine is wrapped up in
Creation, as if there was no deity left to transcend
the physical and be a mind and witness for the
unfolding universe. Still, it's a tour de force and
a marvelous challenge to anyone raised in the
West who wishes to embrace the theology of the
East. Check Christian bookstores or call 616-
676-9185.

THE RELIGIONS OF MAN by Houston Smith, Harper & Row. Written before anyone blushed at the sexism of such a title, this is an *excellent* text on the world's religions, written in a lucid and reader-friendly way. Its discussion of Hinduism is maybe the best synopsis I've found so far.

THE PERENNIAL PHILOSOPHY by Aldous Huxley, Harper & Row. Huxley was obviously struck by the thinking of India and set about looking for the most central ingredients of *all* faiths. This isn't a text about Hinduism, specifically, but it discusses the issues of faith so profoundly (without being stuffy about it) that it's an invaluable read.

Another classic in the same genre is William James' **THE VARIETIES OF RELIGIOUS EXPERIENCE**, Penguin Classics. Speaking to a sophisticated and worldly British audience in a series of lectures, James asks exactly what is going on when people have spiritual experiences.

Smith's, Huxley's and James' books are wonderful experiences for anyone who has never studied theology before and has decided to begin. I'd recommend reading them in the order of their listing here.

THE ART OF SEXUAL ECSTACY - the path of sacred sexuality for western lovers by Margo Anand, Tarcher Publications. This is a beautifully illustrated book about how to love souls through their bodies (with yours.) Those on the Path of Renunçiation need not bother with this one, but those who wish to do the things they're already doing in a more spiritual way could learn a lot.

There is a wide variety of books available on the various schools of Yoga. Here is a very short list of good ones.
HOW TO USE YOGA by Mire Mehta, Anness Pub. Ltd. 1 Boundary Row London UK. SEI 8HP
KUNDALINI YOGA, guidelines for Sadhana by Yogi Bhajan, Arcline Pubs.

Likewise, there are lots of books on Reiki, although, even more than Yoga maybe, it is best to study under a traditional master.
EMPOWERMENT THROUGH REIKI by Paula Horan Lotus Light / Shangri La Publishing
ISBN 0-941-52484-1
or REIKI - UNIVERSAL LIFE ENERGY by Bodo Bajinski and Shalila Sharamon, Life Rhythm Pubs.

For a *huge* selection of books on all aspects of Hinduism, contact Bharatiya Vidya Bhavan (USA) at 305 7th Ave. NYC, NY. 10001

I worry that I may prejudice you against many wonderful books for not knowing about them or not mentioning them here. My list is intended as a jumping-off point only.

APPENDIX 2
– SOME GOOD MUSIC –

There's some terrific music from India available in the West. Some of it is usefull for meditation; other music is just very enjoyable for the mood of it... for its own sake There is also good music for meditation that isn't Indian, too.

FOR MEDITATION:

COLORS OF THE HEART, Amit Chatterjee, Relaxation Co. Inc. (very even, sometimes haunting)

HIMALAYAN NIGHTS, Ferraro & Howard, Clarity Music Co. (good floating music)

MAHOGANY NIGHTS, Al Gromer Khan, Hearts of Space Music (some dreamy, some wistfully melodic... possibly a bit sexy in a languid way)

OM, the reverberation of source, by Syncronicity, chants... instrumentation, surf

CHANTS OF INDIA, Ravi Shankar, produced by George Harrison for Angel Records... a nice counterpoint to some of the more slickly-produced CDs, these are traditional chants done in traditional ways

NON-INDIAN MEDITATIONS:

LIQUID MIND, Chuck Wild, C.W. Records, Hollywood, CA. (very even, good floating music)

MAJESTY... ANGEL LOVE... by Aeoliah, Helios Enterprises (heavenly is a good word... has a slow breathing rhythm to it)

MOODS OF INDIA:

ROOTS AND WINGS, NADA BRAHMA, WEAVING MY ANCESTOR'S VOICES... all by Shiela Chandra, Indipop/Caroline records Inc. (Lots of good meditating material here, also lots of varied tempos in other pieces. Some might find a subtle erotic quality in her voice and many of her compositions. You often get what you're listening for with music like this.)

RAVI SHANKAR, Sounds of India, Ravi Shankar, Columbia Records (This master of the sitar taught the Beatles and explains his music here, identifying instruments and explaining how the ragas of Indian music go together. It's good music plus a good music lesson.)

TANA MANA, Ravi Shankar Project, Private Music Inc. (Mostly lively music, varied moods)

PASSAGES, Shankar & Glass, Private Music Inc. (an interesting and enthusiastic collaboration that works nicely)

SPIRIT OF INDIA, Terry Oldfield, New world Music (good melodies and very rich atmosphere, This is East/West fusion at its most effective)

KAMASUTRA, by Shah, Eversongs label, Germany... based on ragas by Chandra Kauns and Jog, intended to enhance sensual experiences. You be the judge.

SOUND-TRACKS:
KAMA SUTRA, Mychael Danna, TVT Inc. Varied moods, some lively, some urgent, some languid, most are haunting with an erotic under-current.

LITTLE BUDDHA, Ryuichi Sakamoto, Milan Entertainment Co. (haunting and majestic, varied moods and tempos; the final piece is an aria of operatic beauty.)

AND...
If you remember the 60s, the music of India made a huge impact on popular music. The Beatles studied under Ravi Shankar, for example. Maybe the finest example of Eastern music in 60s-70s rock is *THRESHOLD OF A DREAM* by the Moody Blues, Threshold (DERAM) Records. One cut, *"OM"* is, alone, worth finding a copy of the recording.

With a home sound system, you can easily make tapes, selecting pieces from various sources for whatever mood you like. If equipment permits, blending in tapes of natural sounds (birds, surf, crickets, thunderstorms, Tibetan bowls, etc., can produce stunning and hypnotic effects – especially effective for meditation. Check out the WORLD MUSIC section at larger music/book stores.

APPENDIX - 3

ORGANIZATIONS OF INTEREST

The internet is probably the best place to look for company. There are a number of organizations around the world that have been in place a long time. Others are new and may not be out there by the time you read this. Here's a starting point. If you found a congregation, why not put out a home page, get something started.

SELF-REALIZATION FELLOWSHIP
3880 San Rafael Ave.
L.A., CA. 90065

ISKON
(International Society for Krishna Consciousness)

THE YOGA INSTITUTE
Shri Yogendra Marg.
Prabhat Colony
Santacruz (E)
Mumbai (Bombay) - 400055 - India
Tel: 6110506/6122185;
http://www.geocities.com/Athens/6709/

VIVEKANANDA FOUNDATION
P O Box 1351, Alameda CA, 94501, USA
fax 510-522-0910   e-mail info@vivekananda.org
http://www.vivekananda.org/

VISHWA HINDU FARISHAD
http://www.vhp.org/vhp/
*various locations

SINDHI VIRTUAL HOME
http://www.sindhi.org/
*group of people

YOGA IN DAILY LIFE
1310 Mt. Vernon Ave.
Alexandria, VA 22301
Tel. 703-299-8946
Fax. 703-299-9051
E-mail: yidl@erols.com
*International Organization
http://www.uni-
mb.si/%7Eustlat02d/Eng/index.html

HINDU STUDENTS COUNCIL
(located in separate sites:)

The MIT Chapter(e-mail)
rahul@ilm.pfc.mit.edu
sasthana@mit.edu

PURDUE UNIVERSITY
hsc@expert.cc.purdue.edu

UNIVERSITY OF MICHIGAN
vmahavis@umich.edu

GEORGIA TECH
Dinesh@cad.gatech.edu

UCLA
Vinayaka Pandit-(310) 824-0257
hsc@ucla.edu

UNIVERSITY OF TORONTO
HSC c/o ECSU
Erindale College
3359 Mississauga Rd. N.
Mississauga, Ontario
L5L 1C6
ecshs@credit.erin.utoronto.ca

*http://www.hindunet.org/hsc/chapter_directory/

HINDUISM TODAY
webmaster@hindu.org
http://www.hinduismtoday.kauai.hi.us/ashram/San
atanaDharma.html

*RAMAKRISHNA-VIVEKANDA CENTER OF NEW
YORK*
Telephone: (212) 534-9445
Fax: (212) 828-1618
Postal Address: 17 East 94th Street, New York,
NY 10128.

HINDU VIVEK KENDRA
5/12, Kamat Industrial Estate, 396,
                Veer   Savarkar   Marg,   Opp.
Siddhivinayak Temple,
                Prabhadevi, Bombay 400 025
                Tel: (+91-22) 422 1440
                    (+91-22) 422 5639
                Fax: (+91-22) 436 3756
                email: ashokvc@giasbm01.vsnl.net.in
                    or, editor-hvk@hindunet.org

Shri Kanchi Kamakoti Peetham(virtual centre)
www.kamakoti.org

CHINMAYA MISSION WEST
United States Centers:
Ann Arbor	(313) 663-8912
Austin	(512) 255-6786
Boston	(508) 470-2661
Buffalo	(716) 662-8457
Chicago	(708) 654-3370
Dallas/Fort Worth	(214) 437-6318
Houston	(713) 568-9520
Los Angeles	(714) 991-KASI
Michigan	(313) 695-0188
Middle Georgia	(912) 922-9710
New York	(718) 671-2663
Orlando	(407) 699-7331
Tri-State (NY,NJ,PA)	(215) 396-0787
Pittsburgh	(412) 366-3022
San Diego	(619) 793-1266
San Jose & San Francisco	(408) 998-2793
Seattle	(206) 747-7288

CHINMAYA MISSIONS, WEST, cont.
Washington D.C.
(301) 384-5009
webmaster@chinmaya.org
http://www.chinmaya.org/

FreeIndia (company)
http://www.freeindia.org/
(always current Info)

RSS- Rashtriya Swayamsevak Sangh
http://www.rss.org/rss/
webmaster-rss@hindunet.org

Hindu Students Forum in Moscow
http://www.geocities.com/Athens/Forum/1432/hin
dustudforum.htm

Divine Life Society- South Africa
Divine Life Society of SA
PO Box 65282
Reservoir Hills
4090
South Africa
Phone: (031) 822314
FAX : (031) 823248

Mail to: Sivananda@DLS.ORG.ZA
Street Address:
513 Mountbatten Drive
Reservoir Hills
Durban
South Africa

THE VEDANTA SOCIETY   213-465-7114
1946 Vedanta Place
Hollywood, CA.   90068   *(Write for catalogue of publications.)*

BHARATIYA VIDYA BHAVAN, USA
305 7th Ave. (17th floor) NYC, NY 10001

Bharatiya Vidya Bhavan's H.Q. in India :
 Kalapati Munshi Marg
Bombay, India 400 007
phone: 011-91-22-363-0265

about the author...

Lawrence Brown is a lifetime sailor and has published three books about voyaging in small boats. He's published a geography textbook, also about 30 articles in various magazines and over 70 newspaper editorials. The principles from his first book on theology, **HIGHER SANITY**, have been published as a classroom poster and marketed to school systems around the country.

For the past several years, Lawrence Brown has produced and moderated a TV interfaith forum. He has studied theology for the past 30 years and is active in the Universal Brotherhood Movement, an interfaith ministry. (One doesn't have to be a Christian to be a minister.) This book describes his faith and practice as a Hindu.

Bettina Brown, his wife, is a massage therapist and Reiki Master. She's also active in the interfaith ministry. Recently, she taught spiritual healing at *The Center for Women War Victims* in Zagreb, Croatia. Bettina is also the author's best friend and first editor.

The Browns have raised two daughters. Both are grown now and living in Massachusetts.

A Basic Prayer

Eternal creator
Who dwells in all things
and beyond all things,
help us to seek You
and to recognize You everywhere.

Give us kind and patient hearts
to love and forgive one another
and share in your abundance.

For all things come from You
return to You
and are unified in You.

Help us remember,
in the midst of our activities,
that this is always so.

Amen.

Lawrence Brown, 1998